MY LIFE:
CLINICIAN, RESEARCHER, CAMPAIGNER

My Life: Clinician, Researcher, Campaigner

Robert Elkeles

Matador
9 Priory Business Park,
Wistow Road, Kibworth Beauchamp,
Leicestershire, LE8 0RX
Tel: 0116 279 2299
Email: books@troubador.co.uk
Web: www.troubador.co.uk/matador
Twitter: @matadorbooks

ISBN 978 1800462 779

British Library Cataloguing in Publication Data.
A catalogue record for this book is available from the British Library.

Printed and bound in the UK by TJ Books Limited, Padstow, Cornwall
Typeset in 10.5pt Adobe Garamond Pro by Troubador Publishing Ltd, Leicester, UK

Matador is an imprint of Troubador Publishing Ltd

To Arran, my family, and my late parents, Arthur and Margrit

CHAPTER 1

Introduction

I have previously considered writing down the story of my life. I never really pursued this, since I did not consider that it would really be of general interest. However, my mind was changed by an article by Max Hastings in *The Times* on March 21st 2020 called 'It's the perfect time to write your life story'. He referred of course to the fact that older people, like me, were asked to stay at home as much as possible for a prolonged period. Stimulated by Max Hastings's article, I would like to set down a record of my life for my wife, children and grandchildren, and some friends and colleagues who may find this of interest.

Background

I was born on Monday June 1st 1942 at home, 29 Holne Chase, Hampstead Garden Suburb, London.

My father, Dr Arthur Elkeles, arrived in England from Germany in 1933. Arthur was born in Posen (now Posnan) in 1898. He was one of five brothers. His father, Samuel, had a large timber mill. After finishing school, he served in the army in the First World War and was awarded the Iron Cross. He then studied medicine in Munich, Breslau and Berlin. From 1923 till 1933 he worked at the Rudolf-Virchow Hospital. He was appointed visiting lecturer in internal medicine. He was involved in research into gastric secretion and into diphtheria.

However, the arrival of National Socialism put paid to his chances of promotion to a consultant position. In 1933 the '*Arierparagraphen*' laws were passed, which prevented Jews from holding government posts, and he lost his job (Figs 1–3).

A story about another doctor illustrates this well. This is the story of Dr Edith Bulbring, a colleague of Arthur's in the same hospital. This story is taken from the book *Hitler's Gift* by Jean Medawar and David Pyke. She was a junior doctor in the children's department when a boy was admitted with diphtheria. The membrane due to the diphtheria was growing in his larynx and threatened to suffocate him. He needed an operation to save his life. She sent to the Ear, Nose and Throat department for a surgeon but was told that there was none, as they had all been dismissed. She had never performed this operation but there was a nurse who had assisted at many such operations. Between them they succeeded, and the boy's life was saved. Edith was very pleased with herself. However, when the medical director appeared and said to her, "Miss Bulbring, I have been told that you are Jewish," she burst out laughing. The director was furious and said, "Miss Bulbring, this is no laughing matter. Leave the hospital at once." She did and went to England. She became a very eminent professor of pharmacology at Oxford and a Fellow of the Royal Society.

The book *Hitler's Gift* describes the plethora of Jewish scientists and doctors who fled to Britain and the USA, many of whom were Nobel Prize winners and who contributed so much to us.

Arthur was a very proud man who lived for his work, and it must have been a body blow for him to lose his job, and be excluded from work in the German health service. He also had considerable foresight and saw what was going on around him. He realised that there was no future for him in Germany and in 1933 he emigrated to England. After arriving in England, he returned to Germany to marry Margrit Stein and they both then came over to England. I do not know how they met.

He was fortunate to obtain a visiting fellowship, on the recommendation of his previous boss, at the Medical Research Council. He had to requalify. He then worked as a GP in

Muswell Hill, London. Later he trained to become a radiologist and eventually was appointed a consultant radiologist at the Metropolitan and Prince of Wales Hospitals in London. This must have been a considerable achievement. To his huge credit, he was active in clinical research. He made numerous observations based on radiology. He observed a negative correlation between the amount of calcium deposited in the aorta and the presence of gastric cancer. Amazingly, and by a strange coincidence, I also found myself working on calcium deposits in the coronary arteries, measured by computed tomography many years later (of which more later). My parents never spoke to me about their early life in London. I believe they were poor. Eventually they became more prosperous and were able to afford a house in Hampstead Garden Suburb. Margrit was a wonderfully good-hearted, warm and generous person who never thought ill of anyone. Her father was Joseph Stein, a prosperous grain merchant from Dusseldorf. He also managed to settle in London, in Hampstead Garden Suburb, very near to our house. He had with him two sisters-in-law, with whom Arthur did not get on. Margrit had inexhaustible patience and never lost her temper. Unlike Arthur, she was incredibly patient with my sister, Marion. She did give me a sound and well-deserved telling-off on one occasion. I must have been about six years old and we were returning from the shops. She met a friend, Mrs Meyer, and they engaged in long conversation. I became impatient and threw a mud ball at Mrs Meyer. Margrit was not amused. Margrit was the youngest of three sisters, the others being Ilse and Trude. Ilse and Trude and their husbands settled in the USA. Ilse has a daughter, Nancy, married to Brian. I am in frequent contact with them by email. They have a daughter, Elizabeth, who has run a health and wellness podcast (*thatssoretrograde*) for the last five years.

Their first child, Marion, was born in 1937. Unfortunately, she had what is known these days as "learning difficulties". This was the source of much of Arthur's ill temper. He could never reconcile himself to this. He frequently lost patience with Marion, who struggled with school. She was overweight and completely unacademic and liked listening to pop music. She was a huge disappointment to Arthur. It was because of Marion that he channelled all his ambition for his family into me. I was strongly encouraged to work hard and to succeed at school.

Arthur was a complex personality. He had a fierce temper and could be quite unpleasant till he calmed down. He could also be very kind and generous, but he had an inferiority complex and was desperate for recognition by his peers. I became close to him and we often went for walks in the evening together. He never spoke of his life in Germany, so I never found out what went on.

Arthur was one of five brothers. The oldest, Julian, emigrated to Guatemala, where he built up a successful coffee plantation. The youngest brother, Ludwig, was Arthur's despair. He had been an outstanding law student in Germany. Apparently, he turned down the opportunity to marry into the Schocken family, who owned one of Germany's largest department stores. He came over to London and tried his hand at various businesses, all of which failed. Arthur did his best to support him. I really enjoyed his company when he came to our house. He was very good fun, and very knowledgeable on current affairs. We had many good times together. Eventually he went off to Guatemala to work with the older brother, Julian, but this also did not work out. He returned to London but eventually returned to Germany. There, he apparently made a fortune by investing in stocks and shares. He married a German lady whom we never met. He was wealthy enough to be a benefactor to Israel, about which he had never before shown any interest. He endowed some public spaces and an annual prize in medicine called the Elkeles Prize. I was invited to attend the award ceremony on several occasions but never went.

I think our life at home was reasonably happy. We had all that we needed. We had a maid called Ethel Harris who "lived in" on the top floor. Arthur trained in radiology and after becoming a consultant set up a private practice in Devonshire Place (next to Harley Street). Margrit was trained to assist him and she acted as radiographer and secretary. Arthur had a patient called Joseph Oppenheimer, a portrait painter. He paid his bills by painting portraits of the whole family.

Arthur and Margrit were a happy and very devoted couple. One summer, Arthur reluctantly allowed Margrit to travel to the USA on her own to visit her sisters. Arthur, Marion and I spent a holiday in Bideford, Devon. Arthur seemed lost without Margrit. We enjoyed family holidays. We went to nice hotels in England. Later, the summer holiday was usually a drive through Europe, avoiding Germany, to the Swiss Alps. They enjoyed walking, which I did not, and Marion certainly didn't. This was followed by a week in the Italian lakes. We usually stayed overnight en route. I well remember staying at a small railway hotel outside Basle in Switzerland. I was fascinated by the trains and the food was delicious. Driving was more adventurous then compared to now and Arthur seemed to enjoy it. On one holiday we had an Austin Sixteen. This was a heavy car and frequently the engine cooling system "boiled" on climbing the Swiss mountain passes. Arthur thought the answer was to have a larger fan fitted. He did. When he came to collect the car from the garage, he did not realise that on the Continent cars are usually left in reverse gear. When he started the engine, it reversed into the wall.

Arthur bought a new and expensive car, an Armstrong Siddeley, coloured grey with a red side-stripe, of which he was very proud. It even had a radio. We were driving in Northern Italy in the Centio valley. Suddenly the car juddered to a halt. By good fortune, a very good-natured driver stopped and gave us a lift to the lakeside resort called Ascona. We were taken to Albergo Ascona, which my parents thought would be awful. It turned out to be a luxurious hotel. The car was towed to a garage in Ascona. Armstrong Siddeley flew out the spare part, the half-shaft, and it was repaired. Can you imagine that happening today? We spent our week in Ascona, which was a great success.

My parents were not particularly religious, nor did religion play an important part in our lives. They kept the main Jewish holidays and lit candles on Friday night and Arthur sang the traditional blessing. We belonged to a reform synagogue and I did have a bar-mitzvah. They were both very grateful to England for having given them refuge. They were keen to be British. They only ever spoke English to us. They did speak German to each other on occasion, especially when they did not wish us to understand. I therefore never learned German, although I do understand some. My parents had a circle of friends who entertained with dinner parties. My mother was a superb cook and the food that I tasted afterwards was delicious. Their friends were mainly German doctors of similar background.

CHAPTER 2

Schooldays

I went to a nursery school in our road called Anne Mount. From there I attended a prep school in Swiss Cottage called The Hall. The junior school was in a Georgian building. From what I can remember, I was quite happy there. From there I entered the senior school nearby in Crossfield Road. This was quite different. The whole atmosphere was fiercely competitive. On every Friday morning there was a 'reading over'. This took place in the assembly hall. All the boys were seated, and their parents stood in the gallery above. The headmaster, Mr Gerard Wathen, read out each boy's marks for the week in public. There was more competition between the parents than the boys. It was a humiliating experience for those who did badly. The residents of Hampstead, whence most boys came, were mostly highly ambitious, successful people who were keen to see success in their sons. My parents, and in particular Arthur, shared this spirit to the full. Luckily for him and for me, I was on the whole good at school, mainly through hard work strongly encouraged by Arthur. My best friend at the time was called Antony Fine. We were rivals at school and often took the top two places in the class. Our parents were equally competitive. When we went to each other's houses we spent hours playing table tennis against each other. Although I did not play table tennis again after this, I retained the ability to play on occasions on holiday with Arran, my wife, and now with my son and grandsons.

I was poor at football and cricket, which were the main games played. The school used Hampstead Cricket Club and for football we had to go to Wembley Park. We travelled there on the brown Metropolitan line electric trains, which was quite exciting.

My best subjects at school were Latin and Greek, at which I usually came top. I was encouraged by a rather eccentric classics master called Denzil Packard. He had an ancient Morris car in which he often gave us lifts. This car struggled to climb College Crescent, a steep hill leading up from Finchley Road. As far as I can remember, this was all perfectly innocent.

I was a very shy boy and of course very well behaved. However, on one occasion I was caught talking in class. Mr Wathen used corporal punishment and I was sentenced to a 'whacking' by the headmaster. My parents were completely horrified, as was I. As far as I can remember it was not so terrible.

Another incident comes to mind. Unusually for me, I was involved in a fight in the playground and received a hard punch in the eye. My parents were called; they immediately took me to an eye specialist colleague of Arthur's in Harley Street, Mr Hartog. Happily, no permanent damage was done, and I recovered well.

To get to school in the mornings there was a school run, in which Arthur and Margrit took part on their way to Arthur's practice in Devonshire Place, or there was a school car that picked us up. I had a friend called Timothy Jacobs who lived opposite. In contrast to my parents, who were always on time, Timothy's father, a solicitor, was invariably late. Later we made our own way home. Timothy was a good friend, and I was often invited to tea at their house. I loved eating chocolate biscuits, especially the wholemeal variety with dark chocolate, a fondness for which I retain to this day.

There was a green in our road, close to our house, and we often played cricket, using the lamp post as a wicket, on summer evenings.

My parents wanted me to go to a public school. Just in case I failed to get in I was entered for the eleven-plus exam to get into a grammar school. I took the exam aged ten. When I got home from the exam my parents were anxious to find out how I had got on. All right, I replied, I could do most of the questions; however there was one which I did not understand. On top of the paper it asked "What sex are you?" I was an extremely naïve little boy and had no idea what this meant. The answer I gave was "Middlesex", thinking the question related to where you lived. This is absolutely true, and I have told this story many times and invariably get a good laugh from people. I was clearly ahead of my time!

My parents encouraged me to learn the piano. I was sent for lessons to Mrs Irma Michaels, also a refugee from Germany, in Compayne Gardens, West Hampstead. I can still remember the musty smell of the hallway and her flat. Although I think I was musical, I did not really take to it. She also had the habit of rapping me over the knuckles if I made mistakes so I came to dread her lessons. At the end of term her pupils would all be assembled with parents to give a recital. I was extremely nervous and tense and was terrified of these occasions. I was pleased not to have to continue with her when I went to my new school.

The Hall was a very successful cramming factory, whose objective was to get as many scholarships to public schools as possible. In my sixth form of eleven boys, nine got scholarships to public school. I was one and got a scholarship to Highgate. My parents were of course proud and delighted.

I started at Highgate school in 1955. The truth is that I was not happy at school. I regard this as mainly my fault. I was incredibly shy and afraid to participate in the life and activities of the school. I think this was partly due to Arthur's influence. He was only keen that I should do well academically and did not appreciate the importance of outside activities. The school was divided into Houses, on the basis of where you lived, and mine was called Westgate, whose boys came mainly from Hampstead Garden Suburb. We had a really great housemaster called Theodore Mallinson. He knew all his boys really well, and their parents. We would all be invited to the Mallinsons for tea. He did his best to encourage me to participate but I regret that his efforts fell on deaf ears. I had few friends at school. The boys in Westgate who lived near were the rather spoilt sons of wealthy Jewish parents. They were much more materialistic and emotionally advanced than me. I made one really good friend,

Andrew McGill. He lived with his widowed mother in East Finchley. We were both quiet and worked hard. Andrew was meticulously tidy, unlike me. His handwriting was a work of art. There was never a smudge on the page.

I was moderately good at school, still best at Latin and Greek. I was encouraged to specialise in these subjects. I received little education in other subjects, such as history and science. I feel that my education was very narrow. Even in the classics, our work consisted of translating Latin or Greek texts into English and vice versa. Latin is a really good training for speaking and writing English. I found that in later life I was better at writing than my colleagues and frequently had to correct their manuscripts. I achieved the standard nine or ten O levels. My pass mark in Latin was one of the highest ever achieved by the school.

I was hopeless at sports, especially football and cricket. I would have liked to take up tennis, but this was not possible unless you were good enough to get into the team. I thought this unfair. I really only started playing when I got to medical school, and then got into the medical school team. The only sport which I enjoyed was Fives. This was played with a gloved hand and hard ball in a court open at one side with a buttress in the middle called the pepper. It had similarities to squash. I was moderately good but not good enough to get into any team. I often played with my friend Andrew, who also enjoyed it.

It was also compulsory to join the Cadet Corps. We were issued with army uniforms. These had to be pressed and cleaned. All the brass had to be polished. Boots had to be polished and shined. We were drilled and then marched up and down Southwood Lane. There was target practice. I managed to hit someone else's target on more than one occasion. I was generally not the army type and did not really take to this activity. We were taken on "field days" at Raynham, Essex. I hated the smoke from the canisters to which we were exposed. The only thing which I enjoyed was eating my sandwiches, made by my mother. This was a pleasure which has remained with me throughout my life.

Highgate was a Christian school. Jewish boys attended the Jewish circle every morning for prayers. When it was my turn to read, I was so shy that I dreaded this, and my voice dried up.

I did not gain from school because of my introversion and shyness. I never overcame these until much later in life, when public speaking and leadership came more naturally to me. I was again encouraged to have piano lessons at school. I was not interested and soon gave up. There was much music at Highgate. My profound regret is that I did not take up an instrument and learn to play with others. Highgate's alumni included the famous composers John Taverner and John Rutter, as well as the conductor, pianist and composer, Howard Shelley. I was completely fixated on work and simply did not understand the importance of other activities. I do in part blame my father, who was similarly fixated and failed to encourage me to see beyond academic work. Thus, I did not participate in what was on offer at school. Only in later life did it dawn on me how important it is to have other interests. At the age of fifty-nine I took up the cello and have really enjoyed this (more of this later).

My school days were not happy. I think that this was largely my own fault. I was in the classical sixth form. Our main teacher was the Rev Charles Benson, or Charlie B, as he was known. He excelled in Latin and Greek grammar, which also became my favourites. Once again, we really did not learn about Roman or Greek culture even though ancient history was one of the subjects. Teaching was geared to achieve entrance or a scholarship to Oxford or Cambridge. On the basis of my A levels, I was offered a provisional place at Balliol College, Oxford, to read Greats, or classics. Although I enjoyed classics, I was influenced in part because I realised that my father had dominated my life and I was beginning to want to pursue a career other than medicine. However, I started to wonder how I would earn a living with classics. I did not realise that I could likely get a good career in the civil service and that classics was good training for a number of areas. I thought that I might be unemployable. Another classics teacher, Mr Tommy Twiddell, had a nephew who was a doctor and talked to me a good deal about him. It was partly this, and the intense medical background at home, that made me change course. I decided not to go to Oxford. I applied to take a scholarship to London University in classics to read medicine. I succeeded in being awarded the Ken Clifford Scholarship and got a place at the Middlesex Hospital Medical School. In retrospect, others would have gone to Oxford and changed subjects while there. However, I was not the adventurous type. My parents were of course delighted that I chose medicine, and also that I would not be leaving home as yet.

CHAPTER 3

Medical School

I started at the Middlesex Hospital Medical School in Mortimer Street. The hospital itself was an imposing building, now demolished and rebuilt as an office block. The medical school was in a modern block, recently erected in Cleveland Street, called the Windeyer building, named after the dean at the time, Sir Brian Windeyer. I started on the 1st MB course. This was for those who, like me, had not done science. The course crammed physics, chemistry and biology into one year. This was a tall order. I was the youngest on the course. Most were mature students from various walks of life. There was a geologist, a professor of Russian, a businessman and lawyer and others. Many had done some science but not all three subjects. For me it was really a continuation of school in that I lived at home and went in daily to the lectures and practicals. I worked hard and was able to keep up with the others. I became friendly with Paul (Rory) Vassal Adams. He lived in his father's flat in Baker Street. The family home was in Medmenham near Henley. He had a motorbike; he would take me on it and we rode down to Medmenham. This was a new experience for me. My work was rather untidy. Paul was quite lazy but tidy and often copied my work, making a much neater job and getting better marks! After graduation, Paul entered the Navy and left with the rank of surgeon lieutenant commander. He became a lecturer in anatomy at Charing Cross Medical School, carrying out research into cardiac nerve conducting tissues. He also became a noted expert on Victorian watercolour paintings. He was obviously a multi-talented man but unfortunately took his own life in 1983. Another fellow student was Louis Herzberg. He had been a lawyer. He was also rather lazy. He was married to Brenda, a psychiatrist. He had the annoying habit of pretending to give you viva and then picking up all your knowledge. This was rather galling, and others also found this irritating.

I passed 1st MB and proceeded to the 2nd MB course of anatomy, physiology and biochemistry. Anatomy was taught by Professor Edrich Walls, a Scotsman with a twinkle in his eye. He was a highly gifted artist who drew the most beautiful and detailed anatomical diagrams on the blackboard. In those days, dissection of cadavers was part of the course. I was untidy and useless and the despair of my dissecting partners, especially David Evans, who later became a plastic surgeon. Another student in the year was Michael Adler. He was a big man and attractive to women. He was not the most academic in the year. However, later he was highly successful and became a professor of sexually transmitted disease and was a pioneer in the AIDS field. He married Margaret Jay, Jim Callaghan's daughter, who became Baroness Jay of Paddington. I started to play tennis and became sufficiently good to play in one of the medical school teams. I made another close friend. He was Peter Hubner. He lived at home with his parents in Golders Green. He was a religious and truly believing Roman Catholic. There was at that time an important Catholic community in Golders Green. We had many in-depth discussions about religion and the meaning of life. We started a small group who met to discuss religion and spent time discussing these matters. His father was a refugee from Czechoslovakia and an antique dealer. Peter also worked very hard. He became an eminent cardiologist and headed up the cardiac department at the Groby Road Hospital, Leicester. We were very close as students and I greatly admired his faith. He married Sandra, a paediatric nurse, and they had a very happy life together. We did not see much of them in later years, but we remained close in spirit. In October 2018, Peter, having bought himself a new bike, was trying to climb a steep hill and was found unconscious by the side of the road. Ironically, he had suffered a massive heart attack and was taken to his own unit, where he died. He was one of the world's truly good people and I felt his loss deeply.

I passed 2nd MB. I was disappointed at the time not to have done well enough to be considered to undertake a BSc. However, this meant that I could proceed to the clinical part of the course. After an introductory course we were attached to various medical and surgical 'firms'. The structure of medicine in those days would be unrecognisable in today's world. At the top was the consultant. Consultants in those days were demigods and extremely powerful. Our careers depended on them and the reference which they gave us. When the consultants did their ward rounds, they would usually be greeted at the entrance to the ward by the ward sister, who would then go round with him (there were almost no female consultants). All patients would be on or beside their beds. The consultant would be accompanied by his staff of senior registrar, registrar, sometimes a senior house officer, and the house officer and medical students attached to the firm. It could be difficult for the patient to speak to the consultant.

The first firm which I did was a cardiology firm. The senior consultant was Dr Davis Evan Bedford. He had a fearsome reputation. The staff were all scared of him. If there were workmen drilling outside the hospital and making a noise which interfered with him listening to the heart, someone would be dispatched outside, and they would stop. He had no time for any psychological problems. If any patient had what he called 'neurotic ill health' (or NIH) he would send them away. On one of our first ward rounds we came to a girl lying on her bed. She apparently had an atrial septal defect. He asked her, "What are you complaining of, young lady?" She said, "Nothing, sir." He turned to me and said, "Young man, what do you make of that?" I replied somewhat naively, "She has not got NIH, sir." The staff looked at me as though I were quite mad, but Evan Bedford found this most amusing and this endeared me to him. In fact, he was one of the pioneers of modern cardiology.

The other cardiologist was Dr Walter Somerville. He was a flamboyant man, immaculately dressed, who wore a fresh carnation in his lapel each day. His car was a Mercedes coupé, registration number WS 4444, which was the phone number of the London Clinic. He was a kind man and a good teacher who made one point on each ward round which stuck in my memory.

Hospital life then was a league away from that of today. Consultant teams or firms had their own ward with their ward sister and nursing staff. Today consultants are just members in a team. They do not have allocated wards or beds and junior staff work in shifts so that they do not really get to know the consultants. In the later years of my consultant life, it was a major achievement if you could find a nurse to accompany you on a ward round. This of course led to poor communication between doctors and nurses. Many of the consultants were larger-than-life characters and some behaved in a manner which would be totally unacceptable today. Nevertheless, the firm structure as it was promoted a sense of working in a team. The staff, both medical, nursing and also social work, worked closely together and the medical students attached to the firm became part of the team and learnt by dealing with the patients at first hand. Today the students move from one teaching session to another and never get to know the patients. Trying to get a student to clerk and present a patient on ward round today is almost impossible. Of course, in my student days patients spent much longer in hospital. Today the turnover is rapid, and they are discharged as soon as possible or sooner.The next medical firm to which I was attached was that of Drs Arthur Wilcox and John Nabarro. Arthur Wilcox was a delightful old-fashioned general physician. He was kind and good-natured. John Nabarro was very different. He was a small driven man with a moustache. He worked seven days per week. His knowledge of medicine was encyclopaedic. I will say more about him later. His speciality was diabetes and endocrinology. He expected his staff to work hard and be present at all hours. Above all, he expected the medical students on his firm to know and be completely up to speed with the progress of the patients whom they had been allocated. If a student on a ward round had not clerked his or her patient, John Nabarro would throw him or her off the firm. This would be inconceivable today. Today it is almost impossible to find a student who knows anything about a patient. I think that for the students, the close links to the patients were a great way to learn medicine, to learn to talk to patients and to deal with people. This skill is so often lacking today. Students today have to be taught 'communication skills'. John Nabarro led by example. He knew all about his patients, and their families, work, living circumstances etc. He would sit down on the bed with each and talk to them as people. He was probably the most outstanding physician I ever met.

I was already convinced that I wanted to be a physician and John Nabarro inspired me to be interested in diabetes. After the medical firms we went on to do surgical firms. We were sent to the Central Middlesex Hospital in Park Royal. At that time, several district general hospitals were famous in their own right; the Central Middlesex was one. It had a pioneering gastroenterology unit under Sir Francis Avery Jones. Dr Richard Asher was a consultant physician who challenged conventional teaching. He described the psychiatric disorder which could accompany an underactive thyroid gland (myxoedema madness) and Munchausen syndrome, a mental disorder in which a person repeatedly and deliberately acts as if he or she has a physical or mental illness when he or she is not really sick. He described 'the dangers of going to bed' in which he wrote about the dangers of prolonged bed rest, which was frequently used at that time in the belief that patients needed it to recover. He wrote several books, including *Richard Asher Talking Sense.* He was the father of the actress Jane Asher. Dr Keith Ball, a cardiologist, was one of the pioneers in campaigning against smoking and founded ASH, Action on Smoking and Health. Dr Horace Joules was a chest physician with an interest in TB who strongly supported the foundation of the NHS and had an important interest in public health.

Another example of such an important district general hospital was the Whittington, on Highgate Hill, which had an outstanding postgraduate teaching programme. These famous hospitals as independent institutions are now history.

I was attached to the surgical firm of Messrs Illtyd James and JG Roberts. Both were neurosurgeons who also did general surgery. This would be unheard of today, and certainly at a district general hospital.

Having completed my surgical firms, we then had a period of training in the specialities, such as dermatology, neurology, orthopaedics etc. Due to an administrative error I missed out on neurology teaching altogether. During an elective period, I attended the Whittington Hospital with the neurologist Dr Michael Ashby, whom I found rather unfriendly and unhelpful. This was a pity, because I missed out on the teaching of the great Middlesex neurologist, Dr Michael Kremer. In the end I taught myself and became quite adept at neurological examination. Speciality teaching was mainly based on outpatients and was extremely patchy. Not many of the consultants took their teaching seriously. The outstanding exception was John Nabarro. The other highlight of teaching at the Middlesex was pathology. The post-mortem demonstrations, which were always packed out, and lectures by Drs AD Cotton and Drew Thomson, made morbid anatomy come alive, so we learnt a huge amount from them. In the main we were left to learn ourselves. With some equally keen friends I attended lectures elsewhere. The Royal Army Medical College in Millbank (which later became the Tate Gallery) put on a series of stimulating early evening lectures which were advertised in the British Medical Journal. With some friends I also attended the teaching rounds at the London Jewish Hospital in the East End on Sunday mornings, in which interesting cases were discussed. I was becoming increasingly fascinated with medicine.

Towards the end of the course students often did a student locum. In this role they stood in for a house officer on leave. This was encouraged by the medical school. It would not occur today. It gave us some practical experience before qualifying. I went to Colchester to do a medical house officer locum. However, when I arrived, they had no surgical house officers and asked me to do a surgical house officer locum. This was a whole new experience for me. I had, for example, never put up an intravenous drip. There was a senior registrar from St Thomas's who was very arrogant. On our first ward round, which was a post-operative round, we came to a lady who reported that she had chest pain. The senior registrar dismissed this symptom as unimportant. It did not seem so to me but of course I was very junior and inexperienced. "Are you sure about this?" I asked. "It does not sound right to me." At 4am I was woken to be asked to see this lady who was in crashing pulmonary oedema (heart failure) following a heart attack. I had to get the duty medical registrar to help. By coincidence his name was Dr Peter Adler, the son of a GP friend of my father. She did survive. I do not think the senior registrar ever acknowledged his mistake.

I passed my final exams and proceeded to qualify as a doctor at the age of twenty-two, which in retrospect I think was too young. There were also prizes to be won. I entered for the medicine prize, which took the form of a clinical examination. I won the Harold Boldero Prize in medicine, of which I was very proud.

CHAPTER 4

The Junior Doctor

House surgeon

The system for obtaining training jobs was very different in 1965, when I qualified, to that of today. The first job was called a pre-registration house job. The newly qualified doctor had to spend six months each in a medical and surgical job. It did not matter in which order. After the first year he or she could be registered as a doctor. Nowadays there are nationally based schemes which place every doctor and ensure that the requisite training is provided. In those days, each medical school had a number of house jobs for which you could apply. Once these were filled, the medical school had affiliations with various district general hospitals, which had jobs for which you could also apply, but you were left to your own devices to find them and apply. The system at the Middlesex was that you were expected to apply for all the house jobs, both medical and surgical. However, if you got one you were unlikely to get two. I was intent on doing medicine as a career rather than surgery. Naively I reckoned that because I had won the prize for medicine I should get a medical job, and only applied for the medical jobs. I was disappointed because I did not get any of the jobs. So, I was faced with the task of finding my first job. Luckily for me my father had a friend, Dr Loewenthal, a pathologist at Chase Farm Hospital in Enfield. He thought that there might a surgical job for me. I borrowed my mother's car and drove there. I was rewarded by being offered the post of house surgeon to Mr Max Pemberton. Whether or not Dr Loewenthal had any influence in me getting it, I do not know. Anyhow I am very grateful to him for the introduction. Thus started my medical career.

Chase Farm Hospital was a busy district general hospital in Enfield. It served a mixed population of fairly poor people and the wealthy residents of places like Cuffley. My role was first to admit the patients, 'clerking' them; that is, checking their history, examining them and arranging any necessary investigations. In addition, I had to assist in the operating theatre. Max Pemberton did both general surgery and urology. An additional role in this job was once per week to act as casualty officer. In those days the current Accident and Emergency (A&E) departments were known as casualty departments. These were usually the Cinderella departments of the hospital and certainly did not have the same importance in the hospital as those today. A&E was not considered to be a career.

I had a room in which to sleep when I was on duty. When I was off, I continued to live at home. Max Pemberton was a genial and good-hearted consultant with whom I struck a good relationship. I am not sure how good a surgeon he was. He sometimes carried out operations, lasting many hours, to remove the pancreas in cases of pancreatic cancer. I sometimes had to hold up the *Gray's Anatomy* textbook so that he could remind himself of the anatomy. Once the Greek anaesthetist got so bored with the length of the operation that he let down the table, leaving us all holding our instruments in mid-air! Max was eccentric, to say the least. On occasion I would be in casualty, up to my eyes dealing with patients, when he would appear and demand that I appear on the tennis court. This would be inconceivable today and rightly so. Doing casualty for the first time was hugely stressful for me as I had never done anything like it before. Luckily for me, there were some experienced and sympathetic casualty sisters whom I could ask. I had my textbooks on hand and somehow coped. It was a very steep learning curve. I also became adept at dealing with elderly men with urinary retention, and at inserting urinary catheters to relieve them. I became experienced in diagnosing patients with an 'acute abdomen'.

On the firm was a senior registrar called Peter Knipe. To watch him operate was an aesthetic experience. He was so deft with his fingers. He was also an extremely good colleague and teacher. He showed me how to perform an appendicectomy. He then allowed me to carry out this operation with him waiting in the side room. I successfully undertook a few under his supervision. Watching Peter operate was such a joy that I came in specially on one of my evenings off to watch him operate on an emergency. Working with Peter was such a pleasure that I almost wanted to become a surgeon. However, I realised that my practical skills and manual dexterity were not up to it. I was still really a physician at heart. Max Pemberton would visit the local cottage hospital. He knew I was interested in medicine. He would ring me to ask for my opinion on blood test results, which was very flattering. He disliked Peter Knipe, of whose operating skills I think he was jealous. He called me into his office one day and said that he could not stand him. He then proceeded to give me an expensive pair of leather gloves.

During my six months at Chase Farm, I learnt a huge amount and much about dealing with patients, which I really enjoyed. I also at long last began to acquire some much-needed life experience, including getting to know some of the nurses. Max Pemberton told me that I had been the best house surgeon he had ever had and that he would ensure I got my medical job at the Middlesex. He did and my next job was working for my great hero, John Nabarro.

Working back at the Middlesex for John Nabarro was a completely different experience. John Nabarro came from a famous Sephardic Jewish family. His cousin was Gerald Nabarro, the flamboyant Conservative MP, who was known for his several cars with number plates NAB 1 and 2 etc. John was the complete opposite and I do not think the two were on speaking terms. John was married to Joan, a sexually transmitted disease specialist. Their son David is an important figure in public health and in the WHO. John had converted to Christianity and was a devout churchgoer. He was a small, fierce man with a moustache. He would see all his patients, both NHS and private, in the Woolavington Wing every day, sometimes twice. As his houseman, there was no formal time off; you were expected to be there all the time. John Nabarro had an encyclopaedic knowledge of medicine and was, in retrospect, the greatest physician I ever met. He took his teaching very seriously and did a Saturday morning postgraduate ward round. He wrote a book on laboratory measurement known as chemical pathology. He carried out measurements of some blood hormones, e.g. steroid hormones, himself, in his laboratory. He also ran a research group with interests in diabetes and endocrinology. The research was based on the new science of immunoassay, which was a new technique for measurement of hormones, especially in blood. He attracted some of the best young people in the field. Examples are Peter Sonksen, who became professor of endocrinology at St Thomas's Medical School, and Clara Lowy, who became an expert on diabetes and pregnancy, also at St Thomas's. Among others was the late Robert Turner, who turned out to be one of the great pioneers in diabetes research. Robert went on to Oxford. There he put together and masterminded the world famous UKPDS (United Kingdom Prospective Diabetes Study). This study was really the first in the world to show that control of blood glucose levels in people with Type 2 diabetes reduced the incidence of complications. This was a huge multicentre study lasting many years. It was extremely difficult to fund and Robert Turner fought against many obstacles to sustain it. The results of this study changed the way in which people with Type 2 diabetes were treated. Sadly, Robert Turner died suddenly at a meeting to present some of the findings of this work. I mention this because Robert Turner was one of several who learnt from John Nabarro and went on to be leaders in the field.

My job under John Nabarro was busy. I looked after all his patients, both NHS and private. There were no regular on take days but patients needing admission would come into our ward if beds were available. Although there was a senior registrar, the first one, John Hearnshaw, was lazy and it was difficult to get him to see any patients. I do not know how John Nabarro tolerated him. The second was Hugh Baron, who was a gastroenterologist, not interested in diabetes or endocrinology but a good general physician. Thus, it was mainly me and John Nabarro who dealt with the patients. I was also responsible for the prescription of insulin for all the diabetic patients in the hospital. I therefore became expert at this. Some patients I remember to this day. One day John admitted an elderly lady, who he said was terminally ill, probably with cancer. When I examined her, I wondered whether she might have the recently described condition of 'apathetic thyrotoxicosis'. In this condition some elderly people with an overactive thyroid gland, instead of displaying the usual signs, become withdrawn and apathetic. I suggested to John Nabarro that we check her thyroid function. He dismissed the idea. I did the tests anyhow and was proved correct. He was impressed. I was also involved in the care of a young lady with Type 1 diabetes who had rapidly advancing diabetic eye disease (retinopathy), from which she would lose her sight. This was before the days of laser treatment. There was some evidence that removal of the pituitary gland might halt the progress of this devastating complication. Accordingly, our neurosurgeon removed her pituitary. The aftercare was complex and involved me being up the whole night with Arthur Miller, the chemical pathologist, checking her blood sugar at half-hourly intervals. This was a drastic treatment which had serious side effects, and happily, was superseded in later years by the advent of laser treatment, which was far more effective and did not have the systemic side effects.

My six months under John Nabarro were a really great experience. Indeed, it became my ambition to emulate him and I modelled my career on his example, which was of a really great all-round physician, expert in diabetes and endocrinology, and a productive medical researcher.

There was a round of prestigious senior house officer jobs in London at the Royal Brompton, Hammersmith and National Hospital, Queen Square, which, if one was appointed, would be an important step to a career in medicine. I was lucky enough to get a job at the Brompton. Here I worked for three consultants: Professor Guy Scadding, and Drs Ken Citron and Reggie Bignall. Guy Scadding was the leading academic at the Royal Brompton.

He was an acknowledged expert on the disease sarcoidosis. He also was obsessional about the right terminology. He renamed the condition known as pulmonary fibrosis to fibrosing alveolitis. The reason for this was that he regarded this condition as first an inflammatory process affecting the air sacs of the lung (alveoli), which then proceeded to fibrosis. Ken Citron was an excellent chest physician. Reggie Bignall was a genial man. It was a far more leisurely time than my previous jobs, with a much slower pace. Patients admitted did not change rapidly. On a sunny afternoon it was possible to sit on the roof and enjoy the sun. Guy Scadding's ward rounds usually ended up in his office, admiring pictures being prepared for his book on sarcoidosis. The other senior house officers (SHOs) were all very bright. Among them were Christina Lawrie, daughter of Rex Lawrie, a well-known surgeon at Guy's Hospital, and Christopher Williams, son of Denis Williams, the neurologist. Christina was a glamorous young lady and she and Chris soon hooked up. They have been happily married ever since. We were recently invited to their 50th wedding anniversary, an event cancelled due the current coronavirus pandemic. The two academic stars on the house at the time were Drs David Warrell and Richard Thompson. Both were from St Thomas's and both had won most of the medical school prizes. They had both passed their exam for the membership of the Royal College of Physicians (MRCP) early and taught the rest of us. David went on to become a leading authority on tropical diseases, including malaria and snake bites, and ended up in Oxford. He has travelled and worked in various parts of the world. Richard went on to train with Roger Williams at King's in liver disease. He became a very distinguished physician and researcher at St Thomas's and later, physician to the Royal Household. Richard became a close friend, and we remain close to this day. He and his wife Eleanor have been unofficial godparents to our children, Daniel and Jenny. Also on the house were identical twins Ray and Trevor Powles, who could substitute for each other on ward rounds, to the amusement of the rest of us. They both went on to become distinguished cancer specialists.

As SHOs at the Brompton, we were thoroughly spoilt. We met at seven minutes past 7pm each evening and would walk down the corridor to a panelled dining room, and were given a silver service dinner! Can anyone imagine this happening today? During this time at Brompton my father bought me my first car, from a garage in Old Brompton Road. It was a brand new dark blue Triumph Herald convertible. After the Brompton I was appointed SHO at the Hammersmith Hospital to Dr Colin Dollery. He was a clinical pharmacologist with an interest in hypertension (high blood pressure). The Hammersmith Hospital and Royal Postgraduate Medical School was unique in the country for being really focussed on research and academic medicine. I thought that for most of the staff, their research was their main focus of attention, with the patients being secondary. Colin Dollery was an exceptionally intelligent man, a real driving force in his field. He had a large staff of registrars and senior registrars, including Alastair Breckenridge. Alistair later became professor of clinical pharmacology in Liverpool, and subsequently chair of the Medicines and Healthcare products Regulatory Agency from its inception in 2003. He died recently.

The big event of the week was the staff round in which, a SHO, you had to present a case. This was an ordeal as the Hammersmith tradition was to mercilessly pick holes in any case presented. Thus, meticulous preparation was essential, as well as a supportive boss. Luckily for me Colin Dollery was supportive, and I escaped without blemish. The patient load at Hammersmith was not heavy. It was a stimulating six months, and I became interested in hypertension and vascular disease (disease of the blood vessels). On one ward round, Alastair Breckenridge looked at me and suggested that I check my blood cholesterol. He had spotted a white ring round my eyes, a so-called 'arcus senilis'. My cholesterol indeed turned out to be high and I was diagnosed with the condition of familial hypercholesterolaemia. I have been on diet and medication ever since.

After this it was time to get a registrar appointment. I applied for two and got both. One was to work with Roger Williams at King's in liver disease. The other was as an assistant to Sir George Pickering, Regius Professor of Medicine at Oxford. I accepted the latter; firstly because Sir George was a world authority on hypertension, in which I was interested, and secondly because

I thought it would be good for me to get out of London for the first time in my life and to live on my own.

Oxford then was very different from how it is today. It was smaller and less busy. There was no one-way system. I found a bedsitter in the centre of Oxford. I was based at the Radcliffe Infirmary (now replaced by the new John Radcliffe). Sir George was eccentric to say the least. He had previously been professor of medicine at St Mary's Hospital Medical School. He was renowned for his work on blood pressure and was a Fellow of the Royal Society. He had a bad hip and played on this. He used a stick to walk, which he did with a profound limp. On being invited to his office, I was astounded when he got up and peed into the basin. He was enormously influential in British medicine and was said to be responsible for the appointment of many chairs.

He had very definite views on management. For instance, if a patient was admitted with vomiting blood (haematemesis) due to a stomach ulcer, he refused to consult a surgeon and relied on repeated blood transfusions. This was of course before the days of endoscopy. This was a highly dangerous policy. As a result, when such a patient was admitted we had to change the name on the end of the bed and pretend that it was not his. Sir George's ward rounds were an interesting experience. He would take a history from a patient but not examine them. He was adamant that on giving the history of the patient, no technical term should be used, only the patient's own words. There is a famous story of how Sir George went on his occasional visit to the local hospital in Banbury. He got to the first patient and asked him what his complaint was. "I've got indigestion, sir," was the reply. "What do you mean, indigestion? Could you tell me more exactly what is troubling you?" "No sir, I've just got indigestion." This continued for several iterations until Sir George gave up and went on. A voice was heard at the end of the ward. "Calls himself Regius Professor of Medicine and he doesn't know what indigestion is!"

General acute medicine was a really great learning experience. The Radcliffe Infirmary was incredibly busy, taking in patients from a very wide area. The GPs, on the whole, were very competent, wrote very good referral letters and did not send in anyone who really did not need admission. Being on acute take there was like being in a battlefield zone. Patients came in thick and fast and you had to learn rapid diagnosis and decision making. The medical students played an important role in management, putting up intravenous drips and doing electrocardiograms (ECGs). This was a great way of learning for the students. Finding beds for the patients was someone else's problem, and somehow, they were all accommodated. One incident remains in my mind. I was on take one evening and the duty consultant was Tony Mitchell. He was the first assistant to Sir George, a rather cynical man. We admitted a young lady who had recurrent pneumothoraces (air in pleural cavity). I really did not know how to deal with this. I rang up Tony Mitchell to get advice. His response was, "Why are you bothering me?" I was flabbergasted and disgusted. I knew that I would never behave that way as a consultant. I was particularly surprised as he was an academic and, I imagined, devoted to patient care.

The clinical work at the Radcliffe was satisfying. The other part of the job was to carry out research. I found that Sir George had lost interest in hypertension and was now interested in studying the response of small blood vessels to trauma. I was not really interested in this. I managed to get myself attached to Tony Mitchell and his assistant, John Hampton. They were studying platelet adhesion in relation to arterial clot formation, which they thought was the important mechanism behind atherosclerosis (hardening of the arteries); the process behind the cause of most deaths in the Western world. These two had a hotline to the medical journal *The Lancet*, which seemed to accept all their papers which was most unusual. They very generously gave me first authorship on two of their papers, for which I was very grateful and which helped my curriculum vitae (CV).

After a spell in the bedsit in central Oxford I found better accommodation. I rented a small flat in a farmhouse in a village called Frilford Heath near Abingdon. This was much more agreeable, though I had to resist the attentions of the farmer's daughter. I was able to drive in easily to the Radcliffe in my Triumph Herald convertible. The driving restrictions in place in Oxford today were not there then. One of the patients I looked after had a specialist garage nearby. When he found out about my car, he offered to improve its performance by fitting twin carburettors and a new cylinder head. This he did and the car had a truly sporty feel and a healthy engine roar. I had a reasonable social life and went out with some of the nurses. From the academic point of view, I was increasingly interested in arterial disease, which I thought had a metabolic basis. I therefore decided to seek a job back at the Hammersmith. After a year in Oxford, a registrar post on the endocrine unit at the Hammersmith came up. I applied and was successful. When I told Sir George, he said, "Elkeles, you will be a very good physician but not a biochemist." He was certainly right about the latter and I hope about the former. The year in Oxford had been really good for me in every way. I grew up and lived on my own. I acquired good experience in general medicine.

I therefore returned to London. I initially rented a flat in Putney, near the Thames, in Rothermere Road. This was very convenient for walking along or jogging by the Thames. After a few months, by good fortune, two friends, Richard Thompson and David Warrell, who had bought a small terraced house in Fulham, were off to the USA to do their period of research. They offered me the house to rent. I rented their house together with two other doctors, Berry Crook and Nigel Roberts. Berry was a cardiology senior registrar at King's and Nigel was also training in cardiology. We each had a bedroom. There was a lounge and kitchen. I was certainly not the tidiest resident; I changed my sheets and bedlinen infrequently. I am sure that Arran, my future wife, would have been completely horrified. I think David and Richard bought the house fairly cheaply. Today a terraced house in Fulham is worth a fortune. I kept fit by jogging round the streets in the evening. I remember one evening when the elderly lady next door called to ask me to look at her lodger, who she thought was ill. When I went round, I found him dead on the toilet.

I started work as a registrar on the endocrine unit. The Hammersmith was a unique institution, being the Royal Postgraduate Medical School. Most of the patients were of a specialised nature or subjects of clinical research. The patient load was not heavy but the work which they generated was. Sometimes there seemed to be more doctors than patients. The two main consultants were Professor Russell Fraser and Dr Graham Joplin. Russell Fraser was a New Zealander. He was a pioneer in his field. His special interest was ablation of the pituitary gland using radioactive yttrium seeds inserted through the nose. This was used for certain pituitary tumours but also for sight-threatening diabetic eye disease. It was a horrendous procedure which often had serious side effects. Happily, it became obsolete in later years, replaced by laser treatment for the diabetic eye disease and by neurosurgery, radiotherapy and drugs for pituitary tumours. He was a very dominant figure and Graham Joplin was clearly the junior. Graham was an obsessional man, a very good all-round endocrinologist, with a special interest in calcium and bone disorders. There were a number of other associated consultants and research fellows. The Hammersmith was not a happy place. The atmosphere was tense, and people were always trying to score points off each other and show their superiority. The building itself was depressing, with a very long central corridor with wards off it. There were some modern buildings on the campus and a good communal eating area. The senior registrar on the firm was Dr Martin Hartog. He was an excellent clinician, very human and humane. He lacked the ruthless streak which seemed the key to success at Hammersmith. He had difficulty in getting a consultant job but did end up in Bristol. He became a well-known campaigner against nuclear weapons. He was, incidentally, the son of Mr Hartog the eye specialist, to whom my parents took me after I was hit in the eye in the fight at The Hall school. Another really excellent and kind man was Dr David (Alex) Wright. He was doing research on the endocrine condition acromegaly, caused by an excess production of growth hormone due to a pituitary tumour. David involved me in research which showed an increase in serum insulin levels in this condition and again let me be first author on a *Lancet* paper, which was extremely generous.

It was considered part of the job to produce some research. David Wright got me started. I found it difficult to devise a suitable subject. I did then think of a good idea. It was my concept that the complications of diabetes might be due to deficiency in insulin production. I therefore set up a study in which we measured blood glucose and serum insulin blood lipids (fats) in relation to rather crudely assessed complications of diabetes. We did indeed find that those who had lower insulin levels seemed to have more complications. This work resulted in a major paper in *The Lancet* on which I was first author. This was my first important contribution to research. I was helped in this work by Dr Clara Lowy and Dr Andrew Wyllie, a visiting fellow from Edinburgh. Clara became a distinguished endocrinologist at St Thomas's, an expert in diabetes and pregnancy. Andrew, whom I have not met since that time, became a highly eminent pathologist and Fellow of the Royal Society, describing the process of programmed cell death, which he called apoptosis. He ended up as professor of pathology at Cambridge. I hope that some of the experience which he got with us in this project contributed to his later success. I also received some training in working in the laboratory with an Egyptian research worker called Ahmed Kissebah. Although a passionate Arab nationalist, we got on very well and we became close friends. I had developed an interest in fat metabolism. He showed me how to do experiments in the laboratory on fat tissue and I thought that I could pursue this to obtain my MD (Doctor of Medicine, the higher degree). Ahmed was a very volatile character. He rang me once in the middle of the night to report that he had lost his vision. I went round to his flat to find him and his wife, Imani, in despair. I came to the conclusion that he was having a hysterical episode, and sure enough, after much reassurance, his vision returned.

I had quite a good social life living at Letterstone Road. I had one serious girlfriend, Jackie Bush. She was an attractive, lively girl and we seemed to get on very well. Her parents lived in Shepherd's Bush. It was therefore convenient for her to visit me at the Hammersmith. I remember taking her to a glamorous ball at the Burford Bridge Hotel in Box Hill, which we both enjoyed. I know she still remembers this. I also remained a close friend of Michael Dobrin, a solicitor whom I had known for many years. The three of us went on a group holiday to Corfu. At first everything went well. On one hot and balmy evening there was a disco at a local night spot called Charlie's Bar. Another member of the group asked her for a dance. She seemed instantly attracted to him and was attached to him for the rest of the holiday. I was very upset of course, and it was a blow to my male ego. Our relationship more or less ended. It was perhaps just as well, as we were probably not well suited to each other. She eventually married John Rogger, whom I knew. They have been happily married ever since. They live near Cambridge, and we remain good friends and meet from time to time. I found a new girlfriend, whom I met at a social of Campden Hill tennis club, of which I was a member. Her name was Rosemary Hansen, a Yorkshire girl. She drove a black Austin Healey Sprite convertible. We went out together for some time, but I realised that she was not for me long-term and we parted good friends. By a strange coincidence we met again in later life. She married Richard, a friend of Alex Roney, with whom my future wife studied at the Bar.

Towards the end of my time at Hammersmith, my mother started to become unwell. Arthur and Margrit were a very close couple, and Arthur seemed almost wholly dependent on her. I do not think he could countenance the prospect of her being ill. As I was not at home, I did not know what really happened. My father believed in going for medical treatment to his friends. One evening he phoned me and asked me to come round and have a look at her. He told me that he thought she had some kind of 'abdominal spasm'. I examined my mother and quickly realised that she had a massive tumour in her abdomen. My father had completely deluded himself. He took her to the Harley Street Clinic for investigation and she turned out to have cancer of the kidney. It was very advanced, and she already had developed secondaries. My memory of these events is poor. She did not last long. Arthur was, of course, distraught. I really did not know how he was going to manage. He did have Marion at home, who did her best in the circumstances. He was able to retain their cleaning lady. I think he also felt that I was letting him down by not being at home. I realised that returning home would be the kiss of death for me. He developed an anxiety depression which was difficult to deal with. I could offer him reassurance till I was blue in the face, but it just fell on deaf ears. He was convinced that he was short, too, of money, when in fact he was well off, and went round the house turning off the lights. I also felt sorry for my sister Marion, for whom life must have been miserable. She did her best within her limited capacity. Somehow, they managed.

Sometime before my mother's death, having cut myself off almost completely from any Jewish connections after parting from Jackie Bush, I decided to attend a Jewish social event. This was the Anglo-Jewish Association young graduates' branch. The meeting was a talk on the subject of medical experiments carried out on American prisoners. I thought the general standard of debate was poor, but one girl stood out, speaking such good sense. She was also very good-looking and I was immediately attracted to her. Her name was Arran Miller. I got her name and address. I could not give her a lift home since she had driven herself there. Shortly after this my mother died, and I was so involved in this and the distress of my father that I did not get in touch with Arran. She told me subsequently that she had immediately decided that I was the man she would marry. As she had not heard from me, she wrote to me. I replied and we got together. We started going out together and it soon became apparent that we were in love. We enjoyed sunny, romantic afternoons at the open-air swimming pool in Finchley, followed by dinner at our favourite restaurant, called Musto's, near Camden Town.

Arran was studying to become a barrister at Gray's Inn. She had not had a happy childhood. The situation at home was difficult. Her father, Henry, was a self-made man from Glasgow. He had a large timber business from which he had developed an anti-skid surface called Acme Anti-skid. This was made from plywood covered in calcined bauxite, and covered several of London's bridges. Unfortunately, Henry had manic depression. When he was manic, he almost ruined the whole business. At that time treatment was unsatisfactory, and he had no insight into his illness, so that it was very difficult to arrange treatment.

Furthermore, mental illness carried an even greater stigma then than it does now. His wife, Mylle, had come over from South Africa. She had been a very talented pianist but had played little since. She was a highly intelligent lady but was very conscious of their position in the local Jewish community. They did not really get on and there were rows at home. Arran also had a younger sister, Ronnie. They lived in a beautiful house in Ranulf Road on the Hocroft Estate, Hampstead, which was between Kilburn and Hampstead. They had a Rolls Royce and other cars. Arran told me how embarrassed she had been when she had been driven to school in the Rolls. Arran felt bitterly that her parents had prevented her from going to university. Her mother thought she should just get married and have children. Arran was very academic and did not fit in with the other girls at her school, Queen's in Harley Street, though she became head girl.

By this time, Henry's business had had to be downsized to a small factory in Huntingdon due to his illness. I got on very well with Henry when he was well. Mylle, however, did not approve of me. Arran had had a serious admirer, Donald, also a trainee barrister, of whom she probably did not approve because he was not Jewish. Another man was showing interest in Arran. He was one of the new breed of property developers, developing Hay's Wharf. He had a purple Rolls Royce with a personalised number plate, GMR 1. However, Arran was not really interested in him. Although I was a Jewish doctor, which was considered desirable in those circles, I was a bit scruffy (which I am still). In addition, Arran's mother found my father in his depressed state difficult and Marion a liability. So, I was not what she was expecting for her daughter. We were not put off by her. I invited Arran for dinner at Letterstone Road, to be cooked by me. I had bought veal escalopes and chips etc. I fried them all up. As I was serving them, I dropped the lot on the floor. Arran was horrified. "It will be fine," said I, "I'm a doctor." It was very many years before I was allowed to cook another meal. One afternoon we were on our way to meet John and Jackie (née Bush, my previous girlfriend) Rogger, with whom we were good friends. We were due to meet at Baldock station. They were late as usual. I seized the opportunity to propose to Arran and she accepted. Thus, we became engaged.

I was nearing the end of my time as registrar on the endocrine unit at Hammersmith. I was keen to undertake a period of research. This was considered to be part of the training for a good consultant post. I applied for and was awarded a Medical Research Council junior fellowship. One of the conditions of accepting this was that the fellow had to move to a different unit. I tried to persuade them that I could move to another part of the Hammersmith, but this did not cut the mustard with them. I had heard that Cardiff was an up-and-coming place. The professor of medicine was Robert Mahler, a distant relative of the composer. He had done some important work on fat tissue metabolism. In addition, the professor of chemical pathology in Cardiff was Nick Hales, one of the most outstanding thinkers and researchers in the diabetic field. He had refined the science of immunoassay, which is the measurement of hormones in blood and other fluids. He had a team of young biochemists working with him. I thought that this would be a good environment in which to do research. In addition, I thought it would be good for Arran and me to get away from my depressed father and her troubled family. I went down to Cardiff and met Robert Mahler. He readily accepted me with my MRC fellowship to work on his unit. Arran came down to Cardiff to look around. In truth it was a depressing place in late autumn, wet and rather miserable. She nevertheless readily agreed. The downside was that she had just been offered a tenancy in the barrister's chambers where she was a pupil. This was a very great achievement and almost unheard of for a woman at that time, and moving down to Cardiff would mean turning it down. Nevertheless, turn it down she did to be with me. This was a huge sacrifice. In today's world we would probably have found a way of her continuing. However, in those days it was unusual for the woman to have a career. I am convinced that had she continued, she would have become a high court judge. We went down to Cardiff again to find a flat to rent. We alighted on a flat in the centre, off the main street in a small street called The Walk. The landlady was elderly and of fixed views. Although her name was Mrs Friend, she was anything but. We decided to rent this flat and returned to London to start our preparations for marriage and married life.

My father was still depressed and showed no real enthusiasm, especially as I would be leaving London. I think Arran's parents did come round to accepting me. However, we needed to move our possessions etc down to the flat. I hired a Ford Transit van. Arran's parents were horrified when I appeared at their beautiful house in the van to transport their daughter down to Cardiff. We arrived at our new flat. When Mrs Friend found out that we were not yet married she refused to let us stay the night together. I was despatched to the flat upstairs. We overcame this by putting up a barricade on the stairs and did stay together.

CHAPTER 5

Marriage and Croeso i Cymru

Our marriage was arranged for 10th January 1971. It was to take place at Dennington Road United Synagogue in West Hampstead, since Arran's parents were members, though more for appearance and tradition rather than firm belief. In accordance with custom we had to visit the rabbi on three occasions. We found this rather tedious since neither of us really were followers of religion. We also had to attend the Beth Din, or centre for Jewish religious practice, to verify to them my parents' marriage credentials. Without these we would not have been allowed to marry in an orthodox synagogue. Luckily, we had these as my parents had got married in a ceremony in a private house in Germany. The great day arrived. My best man was Michael Dobrin, my oldest and best friend. The ceremony went uneventfully. The wedding celebration was at the Dorchester Hotel in Park Lane. Neither of us really enjoyed this. My poor father looked thoroughly miserable. At the end Michael Dobrin and his wife Barbara threw confetti all over us at the entrance, which upset the hotel staff.

So we were married! For our honeymoon I had arranged a skiing holiday in Austria. Of this episode I feel ashamed to this day. We spent our first night on Zurich station. When we got to the resort, Solden, I realised that Arran hated and was frightened of skiing. I, of course, enjoyed it. Rather selfishly I went off skiing and left her on the nursery slopes. I think she must have thought that she had made a terrible mistake in marrying me. The only redeeming feature of the holiday for her was the evening meal of chicken and chips at a local restaurant. In retrospect I should never have arranged a skiing honeymoon and I think it was one of the stupidest things I have ever done. Arran might well have divorced me for inconsiderate behaviour! Anyhow, somehow our marriage survived. We returned home to start our new life in Cardiff. Croeso I Cymru, or Welcome to Wales, are the words which greet you as you cross the border from England into Wales.

Cardiff in those days, so different from today, was rather a depressing place. The weather did not help. Our flat in The Walk was small, cramped, cold and damp. Arran found that she had to resort to the library to keep warm. She applied for and got a job with the Welsh Health Board. On her first day they admitted that all the numbers on which they relied were wrong. This was too much for Arran, who decided she could not cope with such a system and left. I think this was a pity and, had she stayed, she would by now have had a very senior position in the NHS. She applied for and got a post as a police prosecutor. This she did until 1973, when our son Daniel was born. She was able to use her Bar training and I think the job gave her some satisfaction. Sometime later, Arran's parents came down to visit us. Arran bought flowers to welcome them to the flat, but they refused to enter it. It was not smart enough for them. They did not approve of our living arrangements in Cardiff.

I started my research on the medical unit, which was in the old Cardiff Royal Infirmary. The new hospital, University Hospital of Wales, had been opened and we were one of the first departments to move into it. The department had a number of technician scientists. There was a senior lecturer, who was a pleasant man, not really interested in research but a good clinician. I found that I was on my own as far as research was concerned. I started work on fat tissue metabolism using the training I had received at Hammersmith. After some weeks I got some, what I thought interesting, results. I proudly showed them to Robert Mahler, the professor, and suggested he might like to be co-author of a paper which I thought I could write. I felt great disappointment and dismay when Robert Mahler showed about as much interest as if I had shown him a roll of loo paper. I realised then that I would have to make my own way. Robert Mahler had been professor of chemical pathology in Cardiff. He had the reputation of being a pleasant man and good politician. When the chair of medicine came up there were two rival candidates: Picton Thomas, a very Welsh endocrinologist, and Bill Asscher, a kidney specialist of Dutch origin. The committee could not decide between the two so Robert Mahler was chosen as a compromise candidate. My experience with him was that he was useless as professor. He was not interested in research or anything else as far as I could see. He was certainly no help to me or other members of the department. There was another lecturer called John Lazarus from Glasgow, who had a strong interest in thyroid disease. He also received no help from Robert and we often commiserated together about the lack of leadership in the department.

I attached myself to Professor Nick Hales's group. His was one of the finest medical intellects in the country and he had a group of young, eager biochemical researchers. Among other topics, they were interested in how hormones acted on tissues through second messengers, one of which was the molecule cyclic AMP. Cyclic adenosine monophosphate (cAMP, cyclic AMP, or 3',5'-cyclic adenosine monophosphate) is a second messenger important in many biological processes. I listened to one of the researchers, Tony Campbell, giving a talk on the effects he had found of thyroid hormone on the response to the hormone glucagon, which stimulated the release of the messenger molecule cyclic AMP from cultured liver cells. He found that thyroid hormone enhanced this release. When I heard this, I thought that we should apply this to man. We found that the injection of glucagon in man, which was used as a test of insulin production, was followed by a rise in plasma cyclic AMP. When we did this in the patients who had an overactive thyroid gland the response was greatly enhanced, and in those with an underactive thyroid gland it was blunted. Thus, we were able to describe a test, hitherto not available, to assess the tissue response to thyroid hormone. This work resulted in a publication in the prestigious journal *Clinical Science* with Tony Campbell, another biochemist, Ken Siddle, and John Lazarus. I was proud of this. The test did appear once in the textbook of endocrinology by the renowned endocrinologist, Professor Reg Hall. However, it was a cumbersome test to perform and with wide variability so was not used much after this.

I also pursued my work on fat tissue and tried to study the important enzyme lipoprotein lipase. This was important in the break down of blood fats. It had been studied extensively in rat fat but little was known about the enzyme in human fat tissue. I obtained human fat samples from routine surgery. This meant going to the operating theatre and waiting around. I soon found out why so little had been done on the human enzyme. It was very difficult to measure. I arranged to go to Leeds to learn from the world expert, Professor Donald Robinson. I spent a day with his technician trying to learn their methods. I did not find him particularly helpful. I remembered what Sir George Pickering had told me in Oxford, that I would never be a biochemist, and thought he was right. I was not gifted in the laboratory. I struggled on and eventually, after huge effort and many setbacks, managed to detect the enzyme. However, I could not find any of the expected effects on insulin. I supplemented the work with studies on the enzyme released into blood by the anticoagulant heparin, and work on diabetic rats and on oral hypoglycaemic (anti-diabetic) agents on fat tissue. I eventually thought I had enough to write my thesis. This was all lovingly and laboriously typed out manually on a typewriter by Arran. This was before the days of computers. It was duly bound and submitted to London University. I attended a viva at Hammersmith and was examined by Barry Lewis, a chemical pathologist, and Donald Robinson. They found sufficient faults in the work that I had to redo some of it. This was, of course, a big disappointment and a source of worry that all this work might be in vain. However, throughout my life I have had determination. We had to unbind the book. I completed the extra work and resubmitted and was awarded my MD in 1974. This was a huge relief. This work also resulted in a number of quality publications, which of course helped my CV. It would be unusual these days to have to undertake this kind of work singlehanded. I am not sure how useful a training it was for clinical work.

After some months of living in our damp flat we decided to buy a house. We were introduced to a really delightful and efficient solicitor called Gerald Rapport. He was a pillar of the orthodox Jewish community in Cardiff. I think he hoped he might convert us but was very tolerant of our non-observance. We also met a flamboyant estate agent called Harold Green. His firm's slogan was 'The man who sells houses'. He had a yellow Jaguar, registration number HOU 5E.

Anyhow, with the help of these two we bought a really lovely three-bedroom detached house in a small road called Lomond Crescent. This was off Celyn Avenue, which in turn led off from Cyncoed Road, which was one of the smarter roads in Cardiff. Celyn Avenue was less pretentious and led down to Roath Park lake. Our neighbours were Mike and Kay Smith. He owned the post office in the suburb of Penarth and was good at DIY. On the other side were a delightful Irish couple who had a Down's syndrome child. Next to them was a couple who spoke Welsh at home. The Welsh language was a new experience for us. At this time there was a resurgence of Welsh nationalism and the language. It was commonplace on the radio. Children had to learn it at school. Sometimes the nationalists painted out road signs in English.

We settled down to life in Cardiff. At weekends we would drive to Llantwit Major. There was a dramatic beach with cliffs which looked like a layered cake. We enjoyed walking there and sometimes had a meal at a pub called the Bear in Cowbridge. For a special treat we went for dinner to a restaurant in the city centre called The Harvesters, which was run by two ex-nurses. We also made occasional trips to Bristol and the theatre there. On one evening I decided that we would hire a rowing boat on Roath Park lake at the bottom of Celyn Avenue. We duly started off and then some rowdy youths in another boat decided to ram us. I lost my temper, stood up in the boat and waved an oar around; I promptly fell in, much to the amusement of all. We got back to the shore and I walked up Celyn Avenue looking like a bedraggled frogman. There was a story that the lake had schistosomiasis. Luckily, I never got this. On another occasion we drove to the spectacular Brecon Beacons. We lost our way as the English road signs had been painted over. As I was driving, I realised that there was a tail of cars behind me; everyone else had also got lost. I also tried my hand at DIY. I decided to make a bookcase. I bought some rather nice wood, measured it out and nailed the pieces together. I summoned Arran to inspect it and it promptly collapsed. I had not realised that one does not nail wood together.

We got used to life in Cardiff. I think Arran quite enjoyed her job prosecuting for the South Wales Police. She had to drive to various South Wales towns and got to know the valleys.

After about two years Arran became pregnant with our first child. She was looked after by John Pearson, senior lecturer in obstetrics, with whom I worked when managing pregnant diabetic ladies. He was not a particularly empathic clinician. When Arran was in labour, at which I was present, he called me away to see a patient. Happily, I got back in time for the birth of our son. We called him Daniel Alexander. Arran's mother insisted that we should have help with the newborn infant and found a maternity nurse for us. Her name was Sister Duncan. She was a fairly fierce Scottish lady who called Daniel a 'hoolit'. Arran of course had given up work and settled down as a new mother and housewife. This was not easy for her. Daniel was not the easiest of babies. He cried incessantly. He was slow in his development. Instead of crawling he moved himself by rolling on the floor. He was so slow in developing that the GP suggested we take him to a paediatrician. After examining Daniel, we were advised that he would not be very bright. How wrong he was! We decided to have a short break and leave Daniel with Arran's parents. We packed up the car and started up the A4 (the M4 had not been built). Somewhere around Chepstow we ran out of petrol. I had to leave mother and baby in the car while I searched for some petrol. Happily, I found some and we were able to continue. We duly deposited Daniel at Ranulf Road. I was unbelievably naïve when it came to holidays. We drove to Sheringham in Norfolk, where I remembered having been for a summer holiday with my parents when I was child. I remembered the splendid Grand

Hotel, where I thought we should stay. When we got there, we found it no longer existed. As it was quite late, we drove home again. That was our holiday. My father Arthur surprised us by recovering from his depression. He got himself together and started to live a more normal life.

My work in Cardiff was coming to an end. In addition to the research, I had maintained my clinical skills by being a clinical lecturer. The clinical experience to be had there was excellent. I started to think about my first consultant post. To get such a post in those days one needed some backing from the current boss. It had become apparent that Robert Mahler, the professor, was useless at supporting his staff. The other lecturer, John Lazarus, also suffered from this lack of support. I quite enjoyed life in Cardiff and would have been happy to stay there, though Arran found it rather limiting. In any case there was no immediate prospect of a job in Cardiff. A consultant post was advertised at Northwick Park Hospital and Clinical Research Centre (CRC). This was an unusual job, being five elevenths NHS and six elevenths Medical Research Council (MRC). Northwick Park and CRC was a new concept to try to combine clinical work with research into common diseases. It seemed like an exciting concept. I was not entirely sure that this type of job was what I wanted. However, consultant jobs in those days were extremely scarce and competitive, it was in London, and I thought that I would get little help from Robert Mahler. For the application I had to present a research programme, which I managed to do. I applied and was successful. Our parents were thrilled at the prospect of us returning to London and civilisation as they saw it. Arran's mother was now reconciled to me as a son-in-law, now a consultant in London! So our life in Cardiff came to an end. It had been really good experience for us both. There is indeed life outside London!

CHAPTER 6

First Consultant Post: Return to London. 1974

Our first job was to find somewhere to live. We wanted to live reasonably near Northwick Park so that travelling for me would not be too arduous. Also, we had enjoyed the relatively quiet pace of life in Cardiff and wished to continue with this. We found a brand-new house in a small development in Acacia Close, off Clamp Hill in Harrow Weald. It was a pleasant spot. The house had a large tree in the back garden which we felt added a rural touch. We were able to sell our Cardiff house and with a suitable mortgage our purchase was completed, and we were able to move in. Arran remained at home with Daniel while I started work at Northwick Park and CRC.

This was a daunting prospect for me. I was very young to be a consultant at the age of thirty-two, and very inexperienced. When I arrived on my first day I was greeted by Graham Bull, the director of the CRC, who said, "Oh, it's you," and walked off. In the CRC I had a small office off a small laboratory and a delightful scientific assistant, Judy Hambley. I found the prospect of being expected to produce research daunting. I really had no idea what to do or how to proceed. I did, however, manage to produce some interesting work on the enzyme lipoprotein lipase in circulation. With some technical help we did some work on the liver's contribution to this enzyme activity. We also studied the effects of the hormone glucagon on various aspects of metabolism. I also worked with Professor Tom Meade, who headed the MRC Epidemiology and Medical Care Unit, on blood fat levels and blood clotting factors. I was fortunate to have a really stimulating and dynamic registrar, called Richard Paisey. He was a highly idealistic young man who eschewed driving a car. We did some work together on the effects of drugs used for diabetes on fat metabolism. Richard subsequently became a leading light for diabetes in the West Country and an authority on diabetic foot disease.

So, despite my initial fears I was quite productive during my time at Northwick Park and CRC. I preferred the clinical side and set up the diabetic service. I also enjoyed the general medicine. Fairly early on in my time there was a junior doctors' strike. The consultants had to take over much of their work. I found it quite exhilarating being in casualty, assessing patients and dealing with them. The novelty soon wore off and happily the strike was settled. During my initial time there I found that I often did not have enough to do as the research was slow in starting, as often happens. I used to walk to Harrow town centre and back to fill in the time. I was also called on to do domiciliary visits to patients' homes, and used a second-hand ECG machine which I had bought. I found seeing patients in their own homes rewarding.

Northwick Park and CRC was a unique institution. The idea was to set up a hospital together with a research institute to undertake research into common diseases. The concept was certainly exciting, but it was too near the other big research institution, the Hammersmith and Royal Postgraduate Medical School. It probably should have been situated in an area devoid of medical academic institutions. However, this would have been too far for those in MRC central office to reach. The idea was that NHS and MRC staff would collaborate. Unfortunately, the two sides had completely different attitudes and aims. There were three main NHS physicians: Drs Michael Gumpel, Jonathan Levi and Jim Raftery. Jonathan Levi, whose parents were friends of Arran's parents, was a highly intelligent and competent gastroenterologist with a good academic record. However, he was arrogant and conceited and now mainly interested in private practice. I found his attitude to me as a young, inexperienced consultant unhelpful and condescending. Jim Raftery was a cardiologist, who actually ran research funded mainly by the pharmaceutical industry. However, he rarely appeared on the wards; he ran a locum doctor agency in south London and again, was committed to the private sector. On one occasion I had a patient for whom I needed a cardiology opinion and he just would not come. I found him in his office, took him by the arm and led him to my patient.The MRC tended to be somewhat snooty about the NHS doctors. It became an unhappy place and there was no spirit of co-operation. Within one year of appointment I was asked to become chairman of the division of medicine. My job was to try to bring the two sides together. I was no longer the shy, introverted, tongue-tied boy that I had been at school. I was far more outward going. However, the two sides were not to be changed and the task was beyond me.

At home Arran became pregnant with our second child. She was under the care of the obstetrician with whom I worked, Ian MacFadyen. He seemed to be keen on deliveries at night. Arran was quite rightly unimpressed with the care which she received during her labour. If we had not alerted the staff, the baby would have popped out unattended. Happily, all ended well, and our daughter Jenny was born on 17th March 1976.

1976 was remarkable for a long hot summer. One evening we had a ring at our front door. The owner of the pub at the bottom of Clamp Hill told us that cracks had appeared in their building and that he considered that the large tree in our back garden, which was a black poplar, was responsible. This was a shock and worry for us. We consulted our insurance company, who told us that we needed to have the tree felled. This greatly concerned us, first because this involved considerable cost, and second because of the possible effects of this on our foundations. As it was a new house, we consulted the Home Builders Federation, who were no help. We then called a tree expert called Dr Biddle from Oxford. He spent the day carrying out a survey and drilling bore holes. He came to the disturbing conclusion that felling the tree would result in “soil heave”. This meant that the death of the tree would mean that its roots would no longer soak up water and the soil would rise and disturb the foundations. We had many sleepless nights after this news. Luckily for us, Arran’s father Henry knew a civil engineer called John Anderson. He came round, took a look and told us that all houses in north-west London on clay soil went up and down and that there was no cause for concern, especially as the house had “piled foundation”. We had the tree felled. There were no after-effects. Sometime later, our next-door neighbours wanted to sell their house. Apparently, some cracks were revealed. The prospective purchasers called round to our house and asked if we wished to sell. After some thought we agreed. Whether the cracks in our neighbour’s house were related to our tree we will never know. Our own house remains completely fine to this day.

In 1977, Henry, Arran’s father, died. He had been unwell for some time. His wife Mylle took over running the business. She sold the large house in Ranulf Road and bought a smart town house in St John’s Wood.

In 1978, my father Arthur died suddenly. His death presented us with the huge problem of how to cope with Marion. I should explain that Marion was just about capable of simple tasks, e.g. housework, cooking, washing and shopping. However, she was incapable of managing any affairs, financial or otherwise. In addition, she was very obstinate and could be quite devious. She was very obese, and it was impossible to get her to lose weight. It was impossible to talk to Marion about anything serious like her health. She still imagined she was a teenager. Arran was absolutely amazing in her support and competence in dealing with this situation. We sold the house in Holne Chase and bought a pleasant flat for Marion in West Hampstead, in a block called Acol Court. We furnished it and it was just right for her. Arthur’s solicitor, who handled the estate, suggested that we invest the proceeds in shops and property for Marion. Arran, with her usual good sense and acumen, saw the nonsense of this. It would have been speculative and could easily have lost value. We invested the money in a trust with the Westminster Bank which proved to be very satisfactory and simple for us.

Marion managed well, at least at the beginning. Sometime later I received a phone call from the bank to tell me that Marion was giving away thousands of pounds. When we confronted her, she admitted that she had met a young Filipino man called Billy who had asked her to support his family. I put a stop to this by removing her cheque book. Thereafter I had to pay all her bills using a joint account. Not content with this, Billy then proceeded to pretend that Marion's flat was his and tried to sell it. Luckily, we got wind of this. An article about this affair appeared in the local paper. These events were scary for us. Arran was magnificent throughout. When I referred to Marion as being devious, this is what I meant. She would never have told us about this had she not been found out. She remained a major source of worry for us for the rest of her life.

Subsequently she met another male companion called Frank. Luckily, he was more straightforward and honest. He was also of limited mental capacity and had worked as a gardener for a council in East London. They must have met through some dating site. Marion could be quite clever when she wanted to be. She also thought of herself as a teenager. Eventually Frank lost his accommodation in East London. He was a good companion for Marion. He had a married sister in Bognor Regis. They asked whether Frank could move in with Marion. After some thought we agreed. The arrangement worked well for many years and they had good times together. We of course had problems and concerns about managing the flat. We had to get it cleaned. Sometimes leaks would occur from Marion's flat to the flat below, or into her flat from above. All these matters had to be dealt with. However, Marion and Frank were able to shop and cook, have meals out and go to the cinema and concerts and for days out. They even went on the occasional holiday. It became apparent that Frank's sister and brother-in-law were completely unwilling or unable to help in any way. In the event, Marion and Frank managed reasonably well under our close supervision till about 2000, when Frank developed Parkinson's disease, about which more later.

Finally, in 1978, Arran's mother Mylle, while round at some friends', collapsed and died from a pontine haemorrhage. We were informed by the police and immediately went round. She had been a very fit lady with no previous illnesses so it came as a big shock to Arran and her sister Ronnie. The really big headache was how to deal with the business which Mylle was running. This was a relatively small operation with a factory in Huntingdon which made anti-skid panels. A small number of people were employed but the work was important as these panels covered several of London's bridges. The employees begged Arran and Ronnie not to sell but to take over the running of the business. They did. Another headache proved to be the house in St John's Wood. Because of the recession, it would have been very difficult to sell the house. They were advised to rent it out. The letting agent, a respectable company, found tenants who had good references. They were a South African family. When Arran met them her instinct was to distrust them. She put these feelings to one side. Unfortunately, her instincts proved entirely correct. They defaulted on the rent. It proved extremely difficult to remove them. They played various tricks, including claiming that the children would suffer if they had to leave. After much aggravation and legal battles, they were eventually removed, having not paid the rent and leaving a trail of unpaid bills.

Back at work I had been at Northwick Park for four years. I was unhappy there because of the politics and I really wanted a full-time NHS contract. I was happy to do research but not on a contractual basis. I tried to change my contract at Northwick Park to a full-time NHS appointment but with no success. I therefore started to look for another job. I looked at a job at St Bartholomew's (Barts), attached to St Leonards, but it had drawbacks, so I did not in the end apply. I applied fora job at St James', Balham connected to St George's. This would have meant moving as Balham was not an easy commute from Stanmore. Happily, I did not get this job. The successful candidate was the one who was the unsuccessful candidate when I got the job at Northwick Park.

After that, another job was advertised. This was as an NHS consultant general physician at St Mary's, Paddington, with an interest in diabetes. This was absolutely my dream job, at a London teaching hospital in the speciality in which I wanted to spend my life. I knew, however, that this job would be very hard to get. In those days there was fierce competition for consultant posts, especially at a London teaching hospital. The process of applying was far more rigorous than today's. After application, the shortlist was drawn up. If I were lucky enough to make the shortlist, I needed to meet various key consultants involved in the appointment process.The competition was indeed fierce, comprising probably four of the best senior registrars in England. I was lucky to get on the shortlist. The main consultant involved in the appointment was Dr Geoffrey Walker, with whom the new consultant would share a firm. Geoffrey was an unusual man. He certainly fancied himself as the big powerbroker at St Mary's. He was a gastroenterologist. He was a plain-speaking Yorkshireman. He had also been an outstanding student at the Middlesex, winning a number of prizes. He had then trained with Sheila Sherlock, at the Royal Free, who was the leading authority in liver disease. He had a big private practice at the London Clinic and a large house in Highgate. For some reason we got on well together, and I think he liked me and thought that I would not be a threat to him or to his private practice. It was made clear that the new consultant would be expected to do private practice to help look after surgical patients with diabetes in the Lindo (private) Wing at St Mary's and other private clinics. I expressed an interest in this which was genuine. I did feel the need to provide for the family, especially with school fees looming. I also did have quite an impressive list of research publications, which at that time was important in applying for this type of job. This is far less important today. I saw various other people. I still felt that I would be extremely lucky to get this. Before the formal interview there was a "trial by sherry". This was a late-afternoon gathering of all consultants who wished to come and meet all the shortlisted candidates. It was not a pleasant affair. You had to keep your wits about you and try to impress as many as possible without putting your foot in it. I avoided the sherry, opting for a soft drink to avoid dulling my wits. Geoffrey was helpful at this event, introducing me to various people. I got the impression that he wanted me to get the job. The interview itself went well and to my enormous relief and joy I got the job. I was overjoyed as I had achieved the position which I had always wanted. It later occurred to me that some of the London teaching hospitals had a reputation for not wanting Jews on the staff. I never felt that this was an issue at all for any whom I had met at St Mary's, which was in fact a very forward-looking and liberal institution. There were very distinguished people on the staff, such as Sir Roger Bannister, neurologist and the first man to run a mile in four minutes, Sir George Pinker, the Queen's gynaecologist, Professor Sir Stanley Peart FRS, the professor of medicine, and Mr Felix Eastcott, the pioneering vascular surgeon, and many others. I therefore also felt very honoured to be joining them. I had indeed come a long way since being that very shy boy at Highgate unable to open his mouth in public. I was very sorry that Arthur, my father, was not alive to see his son appointed to this post. He would have been so proud.

CHAPTER 7

St Mary's, Paddington

Origins of the hospital and medical school

In the mid-nineteenth century the residents of Paddington were mainly servants and prostitutes. Poverty abounded and so did disease. In 1842, a committee of 106 gentlemen launched an appeal for a new hospital. The committee pointed out that in the district stretching from Oxford Street and the Uxbridge Road to Kilburn and Regent's Park there was a flourishing population of 150,000. Annual mortality of 4500 was greatest among working persons who could not support themselves in illness. It was felt to be the duty of those wealthier in the district to provide for casualties and illness among its poorer people. A committee was set up to help. The Bishop of London offered a three-quarter-acre site near the canal basin. Over three years, £15,000 was raised through donations. The driving force was Samuel Lane, a surgeon who had trained at St George's but found his career there blocked by a powerful clique.

The first chair of the Hospital Board was the Duke of Cambridge (Cambridge Wing) succeeded by the Earl of Manvers (Manvers ward). Prince Albert laid the foundation stone in 1845, initially for 150 beds, though 350 were planned. Building work began at an agreed price of £33,787. Many problems were encountered with the building. However, it opened on 15th

June 1851 and was governed by a board of governors. It had an outpatient department with casualty and maternity units. The Mary Stamford and Clarence wings were added in 1896.

The medical school was licensed and opened in 1854. Over the years it struggled. In 1920, Dr Charles Wilson (later Lord Moran, Churchill's doctor) became dean (1920–45). Through wealthy friends, especially Lord Beaverbrook, he raised money to rebuild the school. In 1933 the new building was opened by King George V. The new building was one of the best of its kind in the country. It boasted a beautiful library and swimming pool. St Mary's continued as an independent thriving medical school until, in 1988, it merged with Imperial College. Currently, the wonderful and historic medical school building is thought to be surplus to requirements and has been been sold off by Imperial College to raise money.

I started at St Mary's in October 1978. The buildings at St Mary's, in contrast to Northwick Park, were ancient, and some not really fit for purpose. Neither my firm colleague Geoffrey Walker nor I had an office until I managed to procure one later. We shared rather a strange secretary who worked in a tiny office on a mezzanine floor above one of the wards. The outpatient block was (and still is) a prefabricated block that was meant to be temporary. However, it functioned reasonably well. My first clinic was a classic (now old-style) diabetic clinic of about sixty or more patients, both of Type 1 and Type 2 variety. Such clinics would never happen today. Times have changed so much. On my first day, among the many patients was a young man with Type 1 diabetes. He mentioned that he suffered from dizziness and unsteadiness on his feet. I examined him and found that he had neurological signs which suggested to me that he might have MS. I referred him to the great neurologist Sir Roger Bannister. I subsequently received a letter back saying, "Dear Elkeles, I think your patient's symptoms of a psychological nature." He was completely mistaken, and my patient ended up in a wheelchair. Although a very distinguished researcher and, of course, athlete, Sir Roger got this one very wrong.

My predecessor was Dr Carmichael Young, a figure beloved at St Mary's. He was a good doctor of the old school. I soon reorganised the diabetic clinic so that we had one for Type 2 and one for Type 1 diabetic patients. Today very few patients with Type 2 diabetes attend hospital clinics. I introduced a system, revolutionary at that time, whereby patients had a blood sugar test on arrival. The other medical staff on the firm were a senior registrar who was training in gastroenterology, a registrar and two preregistration house physicians. In addition to the firm at St Mary's, I had a firm at St Mary's Harrow Road, which used to be Paddington General. Thus, my work in a typical week comprised two ward rounds at St Mary's; two clinics, to which I added a third later; and, at Harrow Road, one to two ward rounds and a clinic. In addition, there were regular on take days (twenty-four hours of emergency admissions) at both hospitals. The ward rounds included seeing referrals from other consultants in the hospitals. In addition, I did two private sessions and a session or more of research. On Friday lunchtime there was the weekly staff round at St Mary's. I also did a regular teaching session for students. Thus, in contrast to my time at Northwick Park, I was fully stretched with work. I think that this was the most satisfying part of professional life so far. At this time, being a consultant meant that one was someone of stature. Ward rounds at St Mary's were still similar in some respects to those which I remembered as student. We were always accompanied by the ward sister, whom we got to know well. We usually had a social worker. I loved seeing the patients: this was my forte. I made a point of sitting down on the patient's bed to talk to them and discuss their concerns. We could discuss their social problems with the social worker. After the ward round on a Thursday we would have tea and sandwiches with the sister in her office.

In addition, there was a consultants' dining room in the medical school with waitress service. This would be unimaginable today. It seems like a huge luxury. It was, however, a very useful place in which to discuss patients, other medical problems, and even research, as well as life in general. Later on, I was to get inspiration for my first major research project by having lunch with Professor Geoffrey Rose, the founder of cardiovascular epidemiology. Today St Mary's has nowhere for staff to eat together in private, apart from a café open to the public in the front of the hospital. In general, St Mary's was a well-functioning and happy institution. There was a spirit of co-operation between NHS consultants and the academic staff. There was enthusiasm for teaching the students and interest in their welfare.

Christmas was quite an occasion at St Mary's. During my first few years I went to one of our wards on Christmas Day and carved the turkey for the patients. This was followed by the singing of carols on the stairs of the old hospital to the accompaniment of an elderly pianist who seemed to go on year after year. Many consultants and their families came, and we had drinks and nibbles in what used to be the dining area. I also used to give presents to all our staff. It was quite a big task to buy, transport and distribute them all. On one Christmas, I had bought all these presents and they were in the boot of my car. I had at the time a powerful 6-cylinder Ford Granada. I arrived home and parked my car as usual in the drive. When I went out later to put it in the garage, there was no car. I could not believe my eyes. I informed the police. The following day they phoned me to say that a burnt-out Ford Granada had been found on the golf course. I went with them to inspect it. It was a burnt-out wreck. There were some remains of medical instruments and a brass plate inscribed with my name. The car therefore appeared to be the remains of mine. I contacted the insurers, who did indeed pay for a replacement. Sometime later the police contacted me again to tell me that the car we had found on the golf course was not in fact mine. Apparently, a criminal gang had gone round the M25 looking for Ford Granadas, which were used as quick getaway cars. They put the contents into another, drove off in mine and then later abandoned it. They finally stole a police Granada complete with surveillance devices fitted.

It was increasingly clear that the buildings of St Mary's were inadequate and dilapidated. Apparently, every new minister of health who was shown around the Praed Street site was suitably shocked and promised a new building, but in vain. Eventually the new general manager, Terry Hunt, partially solved the problem by getting rid of St Mary's Harrow Road. The money obtained from selling the site paid for the building of a new wing on the Paddington site. He was able to procure land from the British Waterways Board. The scheme was approved, and building began in the early 1980s. The new wing, named the Queen Elizabeth the Queen Mother Wing, was opened by her in 1987. At the time she came, some other hospitals had closed and she was heard to say rather loudly, "I do hope they won't be closing this one."

By this time, I had also become politically active in the hospital. I was the consultant member on the Paddington and North Kensington District Health Authority. On the colleague front there had been a professor of metabolism called Victor Wynn. He and his unit covered endocrinology in the hospital. He was Australian originally and very wealthy, from the family wine business Wynns. He was an unpleasant and vindictive man who seemed to care little for his staff and was very unpopular. I will talk more about him when I describe my research. He retired in 1986. The opportunity was taken to reorganise the firms. A new professor of endocrinology was appointed. He was Desmond (Des) Johnston, who had been with Professor Reg Hall in Newcastle. Des turned out to be a breath of fresh air. He was a great clinical endocrinologist and researcher. He got on very well with people. He became a very good friend to me over the years, and we worked closely together. We became partners in the diabetes and endocrine firm while Geoffrey Walker and Hugh Baron, another gastroenterologist who had been my senior registrar at the Middlesex, formed the gastroenterology firm. So far so good, but storm clouds were gathering on the financial front.

CHAPTER 8

Private Practice

I will deal with this aspect of my work next not because of its importance, but because I wish to get it out of the way.

I did private practice partly because I was expected by my colleagues to be available to help them with their patients and partly because I did want to earn some extra money to help with the school fees. I was never completely at ease with it as I was not comfortable with taking fees for my services. I kept my expenses low. I did not have a full-time secretary so often had to collect the fees myself, which I did not enjoy. There were, however, many interesting aspects of it. I saw a variety of patients with interesting problems and from different social strata. Over the years I was privileged to treat a number of loyal patients. The first major problem in private practice was to find suitable premises. As I was only doing two sessions per week, I looked for a sessional house. I started off in one such at the top of Harley Street. This worked well for about two years. I was then persuaded by colleagues to rent a room full-time. This was a mistake and completely unwarranted. There was an ancient, rather decrepit receptionist who rather reluctantly made appointments. I realised that this was an expensive error. After a year I moved to another sessional house run by two ENT surgeons, Messrs Holden and Cheeseman. They were decent people and the house worked quite well. However, after about three years they retired and the house changed hands. I realised that the future of private practice lay in being part of a private hospital. I therefore moved to the consulting rooms at the Wellington Hospital in St John's Wood, where I remained until I retired. The Wellington was quite economical. Appointments were efficiently made at reception. I found that I could use one of the resident secretaries, who typed my letters in her spare time. On the whole it was a pleasant place in which to work. It had the great advantage over rooms in Harley Street in that one met colleagues from other hospitals. I was also helped in my work by Clare Poulter, who had graduated from being my research nurse to being a diabetes specialist nurse at St Mary's. I encouraged the Wellington to appoint her as a diabetes specialist nurse, as which she was a resounding success. She was wonderful with my patients, who all loved her. She started those who needed it on insulin and followed them up as needed, and provided others with education in diabetes, so important for self-management. She was a tremendous help to me in my practice and a really great colleague.

I had some interesting experiences. One of the most interesting was on my first day in private practice. To my surprise I had a full list. The last patient booked at 5pm was a very young-looking sixty-year-old called Neville Gold with a young, glamorous wife. He complained of lethargy, tiredness, thirst and passing excess urine. These symptoms were typical of Type 2 diabetes, the condition in which I mainly specialised. I was surprised to find no sugar in the urine and that his blood sugar was normal. I realised that he must have a raised blood calcium. He looked ill. I admitted him to St Mary's, which I was able to in those days. He turned out to have a dangerously high blood calcium level. We managed to get his calcium down with the use of a relatively new drug. The diagnosis was that it was likely to be an overactive parathyroid gland (hyperparathyroidism). This was usually due to a benign tumour of one of the four parathyroid glands, situated in the neck and responsible for producing parathyroid hormone, which regulates blood calcium. This required surgical exploration of the neck to identify the parathyroid glands, find the enlarged one and remove it. It required an experienced surgeon. The surgeon who normally did this was Mr Mike Snell. We did the necessary investigations; this was before the days of measurement of blood level of parathyroid hormone. Mike Snell was sceptical about the diagnosis and took a good deal of persuasion to explore the neck. He finally agreed and I went to the operating theatre. He searched hard and after some time found nothing abnormal. Then finally he found a large parathyroid tumour. Mike Snell's scepticism of my diagnosis evaporated. God, was I relieved! The tumour was removed, and Neville Gold's serum calcium came down to normal and he was cured. He became a longstanding and grateful patient and usually brought me a garish tie when he came to see me. Sometime later I was called by the eminent urologist Mr Kenneth Owen to accompany him one evening to attend to a Saudi Arabian princess at the Dorchester Hotel. She kept us waiting for at least an hour and eventually condescended to be seen. I saw her at the end and did the examination. I thought to myself how unpleasant and degrading this experience had been and vowed that never again would I agree to any such arrangement.

Another of the chores of private practice in my field was being called on to look after patients before and after operations by surgical colleagues. This usually meant going to a private hospital such as the Harley Street Clinic, London Clinic or the Wellington on the way home in the evening. I had to arrange their diabetic regime, sometimes deal with other conditions, and visit them regularly until discharge. I found this onerous. It also involved contacting their sponsoring embassy medical departments to get authorisation for payment. I disliked the whole process. The surgeon who used me the most was the pioneering vascular surgeon, Felix Eastcott. He was very demanding and certainly got my private practice off to a flying start. I disliked this aspect of private practice. Nevertheless, I saw these patients for many years until I was much more senior and felt able to bow out of this type of work. Having to see these patients in the evening was the main reason why I drove to St Mary's for many years. It was only when I partially retired that I realised that taking the Metropolitan line was so much easier.

One of the benefits of private practice was the opportunity to meet people whom I otherwise would not have met. I looked after the wife of President Zia of Pakistan. She gave us a beautiful carpet, which is still in our lounge, as well as a huge crate of mangoes. I also looked after a most remarkable man, Richard Tomkins. He was the founder of Green Shield Stamps. At that time, if you purchased items in shops or petrol stations you received Green Shield stamps which, if collected, entitled you to a gift from a catalogue. He also later founded the Argos stores. He was a simple, unpretentious man. He had obviously made millions. When I needed money to fund my research programme, he was very generous and donated it. Even after he died, his widow continued to fund my research. Without them, I doubt whether I would have been able to carry out all my research. Another long-standing patient was Ron Hatter. When he and his wife celebrated an important occasion with a large party in north-west London, they asked for donations for my research, which was absolutely wonderful. I had many more interesting patients over the years. These included various foreign dignitaries, the Queen's private secretary etc. I was appointed to the staff of the King Edward VII Hospital for Officers and Sister Agnes. This is the private hospital used by the Royal Family. This was considered a great honour. Seeing patients there was a pleasure because the staff treated you so well and were so helpful. For me, the downside of this appointment was that every few weeks one had to do a week on duty; this meant being available to admit patients. I found that this usually occurred on Sunday afternoons, when I had to go in and see some elderly Kensington resident. This took precious time away from the family and I found this too onerous. After a few years I resigned my appointment there. I was listed in the *Evening Standard* magazine in April 1992 in the list of London's 100 top specialists.

From the financial point of view, because I kept my expenses low, I made quite a substantial addition to my NHS salary without compromising or interfering with my NHS work. I retired from full-time work in the NHS in 2007, which was compulsory at that time. However, I returned to part-time work and I continued my private practice until 2011. After thirty-three years in private practice I retired.

CHAPTER 9

Financial Cuts: the Gathering Storm

The *London Evening Standard* carried the headlines on May 15th 1986: "Hospitals Cash Crisis. Consultants from eleven London teaching hospitals claim today the NHS cash cuts for the inner city have been so severe that the care of their patients is now in jeopardy". In October 1987, Paddington and North Kensington Health Authority reported a likely deficit of £3million. They recommended that the only way to meet the shortfall was to make major cutbacks in the services provided to patients at St Mary's and St Charles' hospitals. The new wing was only partially open and there were bed reductions elsewhere. Thus, elective work was severely curtailed. At the meeting of the hospital medical committee I was asked to form an action group. Presumably I was asked because I was known to be a campaigner. It was interesting to contrast myself at this stage with how I was at Highgate School, unable to open my mouth in public. The objective was to bring to the attention of the government, the region and the public the difficult financial position of the Paddington and North Kensington Health Authority and the Medical School. Other members of the group included Professor Richard Beard, professor of obstetrics and gynaecology (O&G); Frank Loeffler, consultant (O&G); Miss Averil Mansfield, vascular surgeon; Ron Marsh, opthalmologist; Clive Tonks, psychiatrist; and Gary Symons, anaesthetist, to act as treasurer. It was later joined by

Anthony Pinching, senior lecturer in immunology and a pioneer in research on AIDS. Consultants were asked to contribute £50 to cover administrative costs. The first meeting was held on the October 26th 1987.

We aimed to get help from influential people like Margaret Jay. She was a journalist on the BBC's prestigious *Panorama* programme, and Thames Television's *This Week*. She had a strong interest in health issues, notably as a campaigner on HIV and AIDS. She was a founder director of the National AIDS Trust in 1987 and a patron of Help the Aged. We prepared and submitted evidence to the House of Commons Social Services Committee. We described the particular problems of our district. St Mary's was both a district general hospital and specialist and teaching centre. We explained that developments at St Mary's, which had added to the financial load on the district, were the facilities needed for AIDS/HIV patients, and for increasing demands for neonatal intensive care, and vascular and cardiac surgery. We also published a letter to the press. It was rejected by *The Times* but accepted by the *Independent*. It was published on 19th November 1987. For some reason the *Independen*t refused me permission to reproduce it. I will therefore quote from it:

"Emergency in the health service

"We have a duty to inform the public that the fabric of the NHS is crumbling about us. Our health authority (Paddington and North Kensington) faces a £3million deficit despite being prudent and having to cope with a budget reduction of 6% in real terms over the last three years. Over the last five years acute workload has remained unchanged, but the bed numbers have been reduced from 900 to 450 and £7million has been saved in cost improvements.

"Hospital facilities have become so tight that we are virtually limited to emergency admissions. For example, it has become very difficult to admit patients for heart disease investigations and surgery, for surgery to diseased blood vessels or for cancer treatment. Some of these patients then deteriorate and are admitted as emergencies.

"Room for further 'efficiency' savings is minimal and no relief is in sight. These pressures have resulted in crisis management which has replaced long-term planning. Other inner London health authorities are similarly affected so that healthcare in London is deteriorating dangerously.

"We urge the government to agree a long-term plan and provide adequate resources so that we can fulfil our district and teaching responsibilities for healthcare. A plan for healthcare for all London is urgently needed."

The letter was signed by me and other members of the St Mary's Action Group.

Tragically, the day before publication saw the devastating fire at King's Cross station. Thirty-one people died and one hundred were injured. This of course completely overshadowed the impact of our letter. We also lobbied the local MPs: John Wheeler, Sir Brandon Rhys Williams, Margaret Jay, Baroness Masham and others. Some extra money was forthcoming. We were supported by Barbara Young, an outstanding district general manager of courage and integrity. The action group continued to meet for some months. At one point in the winter months, BBC *Newsnight* filmed me outside our then casualty department with an elderly diabetic man who had a serious leg ulcer and needed admission. There were no beds. I got somewhat carried away by the occasion, declaring that this was no way to run the NHS, nor the way to run the country! I was asked by the BBC to appear in a debate on the NHS with a health minister. Luckily for me this was cancelled as I would have been completely outclassed and out of my depth.

The other factor affecting London hospitals was the policy of RAWP (Resource Allocation Working Party) which, on the basis that London was receiving too much money, was diverting money away from it. We sent a letter to Kenneth Clarke in December 1987 explaining the problem to him (Fig 4).

At the same time as the St Mary's action group was working, another pan-London teaching hospital group had been formed and was working. It was led by my old friend Richard Thompson from St Thomas's and had representatives of all the London teaching hospitals, including myself from St Mary's. We published a letter in *The Times* on May 13th 1986 (Fig 5). The funding shortfall in the NHS continued over the next few years and there were increasing problems with getting patients timely treatment. The London 12, under Richard Thompson, continued to lobby actively. An eloquent letter written by Richard to William Waldegrave (Fig 6) sums up the situation well. The group, including me, met Virginia Bottomley, secretary of state, and William Waldegrave, health minister, to make these points. These high-level politicians agreed to see us because Richard was the royal physician. I would like to pay tribute to Richard, who campaigned tirelessly and effectively on behalf of patients. He was a man who cared deeply about his fellow human beings and was a role model for us all. The health funding crisis in London was reported in the *Evening Standard* on May 13th 1986 (Fig 7). The situation in Paddington was reported in the *Evening Standard* on May 18th (Fig 8). Because of the lack of funds, St Mary's Harrow Road, which was due to close later to fund the new building at St Mary's Paddington, would shut early. I was quoted as saying that medical services over a wide area would be thrown into chaos. Over the next two years there were outcries and protests from the rest of the country about the underfunding of the NHS. This eventually so upset Mrs Thatcher that she set up a review of the NHS. This resulted in the creation of the "internal market". The St Mary's Hospital Action Group met in March 1989 and produced a document in response to the review (Figs 9a, 9b).

CHAPTER 10

The Internal Market

The result of the government's review was the white paper *Working for Patients* with eight accompanying papers: 1. *Self-governing hospitals*, 2. *Funding and Contracts for Hospital Services*, 3. *Practice Budgets for General Medical Practitioners*, 4. *Indicative Prescribing Budgets for General Medical Practitioners*, 5. *Capital Charges*, 6. *Medical Audit*, 7. *NHS Consultants Appointments Contracts and Distinction Awards*, 8. *Implications for Family Practitioner Committees*.

The main principle behind the white paper was the introduction of the purchaser/provider split. Instead of health authorities directly managing hospitals, they would decide what care they wanted and then purchase it from "self-governing" hospitals known as NHS Trusts. Hospitals, in effect, would have to compete for patients. It was believed that the introduction of competition would increase efficiency and quality as well as drive down price, as in commerce. NHS hospitals would also have to pay capital charges for their buildings. The idea was that better use would be made of these buildings and that the NHS hospitals would be on a level playing field with private hospitals, with whom they would compete for certain contracts. General practitioners with larger practices would apply for control of their own budgets in order to buy hospital care for patients, compete with other practices for patients, run their own businesses and plough back savings into their own practice. For the first time,

GPs would not be free to send patients to any hospital of their choice but only to hospitals which had a contract with the health authority in which the patients lived. Therefore, patient choice was reduced rather than increased. This negated one of the stated aims in the white paper: 'to give patients wherever they live in the UK better healthcare and greater choice of the services available'.

Thus, for the first time the business ethic was introduced into NHS healthcare. Of course, it had been present in the private sector. For me this changed the whole ethos of care for patients in the NHS. I could see that those disciplines which attracted revenue would be favoured over those that did not. Patients with long-term conditions such as diabetes, or chronic obstructive lung disease, would receive less than those who required surgery, for instance. In theory patients could be referred to one hospital for one condition and another for another condition. It seemed wrong to me to divide care into packets which resulted in fragmentation. I wrote a full article for the *Independent* explaining all these points on Jan 26th 1989 (Fig 10). The government admired the private sector. However, it was difficult and dangerous to care for really ill patients there, and such patients usually had to be transferred to the NHS, which then had to pick up the pieces. I made the point in the article that we needed now to make provision for good quality care of the increasing number of elderly people. To this day this massive problem has not been resolved, despite recurrent debate and discussion. It seemed to me that a far better way of delivering care would be a planned approach. In this, the needs of a given population would be assessed and planned and funded to the level that could be afforded. I could foresee the huge expense that this new market approach would incur, with multiple purchasers and providers requiring input from armies of management consultants. The government's approach was to deal with healthcare by rearranging the administration, rather than to plan for and provide the people and tools to do the job. My article received much support and several complimentary letters (Figs 11–13) but of course nothing much was changed. The bill was driven through by the health minister, Ken Clarke, who seemed determined to be rude to any of the medical profession who opposed these changes. He subsequently became a much wiser and more moderate politician. Incidentally, I had been appointed interim clinical director of medicine at St Mary's, voted in by my colleagues. I found it difficult to implement the cuts in services demanded. I also found the whole market approach totally unpalatable. I had a hopeless manager. I was removed from my position by the chief executive, Neil Goodwin, and the medical director, Dr Willie Harris. They also disapproved of my letters to the press. My removal was probably a blessing in disguise.

In the 1990s there was some stepping back when Frank Dobson for Labour became health secretary. Labour had pledged to "scrap" the internal market. In practice it kept the purchaser/provider split between health authorities and hospitals, and purchasing was renamed "commissioning" to convey the message that commissioners were meant to influence the quality of service rather than just buy what was on offer. GP fundholding, which had only really been running for a year, was abolished, and Dobson discouraged the use by the NHS of private hospitals. Alan Milburn, the subsequent Labour health secretary, introduced Foundation Trusts. These received a greater degree of independence than other NHS trusts and were a sort of halfway house between public and private sectors. They were able to own land, were free to borrow from the public or private sector, and were free to run joint ventures with the private sector and make surpluses and losses, so long as the surpluses were spent for the benefit of NHS patients. In the 2009–10 session, the House of Commons Health Committee published a report into commissioning. It found that the cost of this process came to 14% of the total cost of the NHS, amounting to 'a staggering sum of £13billion per year'. They found that after twenty years of the purchaser/provider split, commissioning remained a weak link in the English NHS. They found no substantial evidence that the whole market process actually improved care. Rather, under this system, hospitals, primary care and community/ social care were fragmented, each defending their incomes and empires. Professor Chris Ham, an eminent authority on healthcare, recommended a more integrated approach in which they would all work together.

Despite all this evidence, politicians remained committed to this false market. There was a widespread belief that many hospital consultants were lazy and too interested in their private practice. While this may have been true for a minority, the majority worked extremely hard for the NHS. There was a reluctance to embark on further changes to the structure of the NHS. I described the effects of competition on the NHS and advocated a more planned approach to provision of services in a letter to the *British Medical Journal* (Fig 14) and *The Times* (Fig 15). I returned to this theme in another letter to *The Times*, March 4th 2013, when there was a campaign to remove Sir David Nicholson from his post at the top of the NHS (Fig 16). I again pointed out that, although it was the idea of competition which appealed to most politicians, journalists and health economists, as a way of motivating people it achieved the opposite and sapped morale. In 2014 (Lord) David Owen wrote a book called *The Health of the Nation*. He concluded the introduction: "In the pick of the week's correspondence from many newspapers published by *The Week* on 9th March 2013, at the time of controversy whether the chief executive of the NHS, Sir David Nicholson, should resign one letter stood out: He then reproduced in full my letter to *The Times* of March 4th 2013. He went on: "Healthcare is not like any other business or utility like gas, water or electricity and I hope this will be very clear to everyone who reads this book." This is precisely the point I was trying to make.

When David Cameron became prime minister in 2010, he promised that there would be no more "top down" reorganisation of the NHS. His health secretary, Andrew Lansley, however, had other ideas. The *Health and Social Care Act* of 2012 would "liberate" the NHS. The Act changed the way that healthcare was commissioned and proved to be highly controversial. Sir David Nicholson, chief executive of the NHS, said the change would be 'big enough to be seen from space'. The government emphasised that from the public point of view nothing would change, with access to NHS services on the basis of need, not ability to pay.

The Act would put clinicians at the centre of commissioning, free up providers to innovate, empower patients and give a new force to Public Health England. 152 Primary Care Trusts (PCTs) were replaced by 211 Clinical Commissioning Groups (CCGs). PCTs had been in charge of buying and providing healthcare for their local populations. This would now be the task of CCGs. While the PCTs were mainly staffed by administrators, CCGs would be led by GPs. Thus, GPs were put in control of the majority of the NHS budget. The idea behind this was that GPs knew best what care their patients needed, so could "commission" services on their behalf. Hospitals would have no say in service provision. I and many others thought this was wrong.

At the time, I was on the committee of the Hospital Consultants Association. Through this we were granted a meeting with Earl Howe, the Conservative health minister in the Lords and the man chosen as fixer of the bill to mollify the fierce opposition. I had also met Earl Howe through the Royal College of Physicians, of which he was a friend and I a council member, of which more later. I put it to Earl Howe that GPs did not have a monopoly of the knowledge of the healthcare needs of a population and that there should at least be some representative of the hospitals (secondary care) on CCGs. This did not seem to have occurred to the minister and I think that I convinced him. The Royal College of Physicians, through their president, my good friend Richard Thompson, also lobbied for the same thing. We and others were at least successful in this endeavour and a secondary care doctor was now included on the board of CCGs, as well as a nurse representative.

In addition, a new body was set up, the NHS Commissioning Board, which would provide advice to CCGs on coordinating patient care. Above CCGs, the Care Quality Commission (CQC) was set up to ensure that standards of care were maintained, while another body, Monitor, would keep track of how CCGs were managing their budgets. The Strategic Health Authorities, which had existed to supervise PCTs and which provided a mechanism for rationalising healthcare within a region, were abolished. Thus, there was now no mechanism whereby services could be reorganised except by so-called market forces. The new system opened up the market to private providers and the Act made the relationship between the public and private sector a more formal one. The coalition government struggled to explain to the electorate why this reorganisation was so vital to secure the future of the NHS. They also had difficulty in convincing parliament. They embarked on a pause in the legislation but eventually the Bill was passed and became an Act.

The NHS continued to run a huge deficit and faced calls for evermore "efficiency savings". The Lansley Bill was meant to reduce bureaucracy and improve efficiency through more competition. This did not happen. Once again politicians had tried to sort out healthcare with process rather than substance. I pointed this out in my letter to *The Times*, January 8th 2015 (Fig 17). I suggested that healthcare needed to be planned like defence, and not left to market forces. On May 21st 2016, Chris Hopson, chief executive of NHS providers, wrote a piece in *The Times*: 'Our health service is running on empty'. He pointed out that 65% of trusts were in financial arrears and that their total deficit was a record £2.5billion. Although some politicians blamed poor financial management for this, he described 'the toxic cocktail' of three problems with which the NHS was grappling. First, there was the increasing number of frail elderly arriving in hospital for treatment. This was overwhelming hospital capacity. Second, there was the most prolonged and deep financial squeeze. Cost and demand were rising by 3.5–4% per year but protected funding for the NHS was rising by only 0.9% per year. Third, 4% efficiency targets had been imposed that were unrealistic, causing long-term damage to Trust finances. Trusts had delivered £19billion in efficiency savings, but asking for savings three times the NHS average would be unworkable. He suggested, as did others, that alternative ways of funding should be explored. In a letter to *The Times* on May 24th 2016 (Fig 18), I explained that large sums of money were haemorrhaging from the NHS through the hugely wasteful process of commissioning. Even before the Lansley reforms, the process consumed 14% of the budget. The reforms themselves cost up to £3billion to implement. Although the changes were supposed to reduce bureaucracy there were now 211 CCGs, each with their own infrastructure, which must have hugely increased costs. Interestingly, Andrew (now Lord) Lansley disputed these figures in a letter to *The Times* on May 27th 2016. In addition, the GPs sitting on CCGs were struggling to combine their jobs as GPs with their roles in commissioning. These issues needed to be resolved by a more integrated approach so that the different parts worked together instead of in competition. By doing so it might be possible to keep more of the elderly out of hospital. On August 25th 2017, Paul Johnson, director of the Institute for Fiscal Studies, wrote in *The Times*, 'The NHS doesn't deserve our hero worship', debunking what he considered to be the myth that we had the best healthcare system in the world. The OECD had reported that, while access to healthcare was good, the quality of care in the UK was uneven and lagged behind that in many other OECD countries. The main concern was the lack of provision and funding for social care.

I replied in a letter to *The Times* on August 28th (Fig 19) that we needed to restore pride in the NHS. I pointed out that the financial deficit of most trusts was caused in the main by the increased staffing costs resulting from the shortage of medical and nursing staff, requiring the employment of large numbers of expensive agency and locum staff. Many doctors in training were emigrating to seek better working conditions. GPs were retiring early due to pressure of work. The NHS was being asked to find £22billion in efficiency savings while money was draining away on the complex commissioning system and armies of management consultants. My thesis was that the market set different parts of the system of the NHS against one another, leading to fragmented, rather than integrated, care. We needed to return to a system whereby healthcare was planned, which would ensure integration and restore professionalism, pride and satisfaction in working in the NHS. In conclusion, my view and that of very many others was that the internal market had been an expensive failure. It had made health workers feel undervalued and de-professionalised. It had not resulted in better healthcare but had greatly increased administrative costs. The Lansley reforms are now acknowledged, even by most Tories, to have been one of their most disastrous errors.

David Cameron did not understand what his health secretary was doing. The changes hugely increased management costs and further fragmented care, having been sold as doing the opposite. Furthermore, David Cameron, having promised that he would not undertake any top down change to the NHS, oversaw one of the biggest upheavals in its history, with no tangible benefits. After about thirty years, the internal market is only now gradually being dismantled. Its demise is being accelerated by the Covid-19 pandemic. What a shame it has taken so long for policy makers to realise what a ghastly mess they created with this misguided, ideological approach to healthcare.

Law for the Restoration of the Professional Civil Service ("Civil Service Law") 7 April 1933

The Law for the Restoration of the Professional Civil Service, or "Civil Service Law" for short, was decreed one week after the nation-wide boycott of businesses owned by Jews and represented the first comprehensive law of occupational discrimination directed against Jewish citizens. With the so-called "Aryan Clause" (*Arierparagraph*) in § 3, the law established a racial criterion for continued employment in the civil service, effectively banishing Jews from government and administration; it also set a model that would soon be followed in other professions. The only exceptions allowed were for persons who had entered the civil service prior to World War I and for Jews who had fought in the German military.

The Reich government has enacted the following law, promulgated herewith:

§ 1

(1) To restore a national professional civil service and to simplify administration, civil servants may be dismissed from office in accordance with the following regulations, even where there would be no grounds for such action under existing law.

(2) For the purposes of this law the following are to be considered civil servants: direct and indirect officials of the Reich, direct and indirect officials of the states (*Länder*), officials of local communities and communal associations, and officials of corporations under public law, as well as of institutions and enterprises of equivalent legal status (see Third Executive Order of the Reich President for the Stabilization of the Economy and Finances, 6 October 1931, *Reichsgesetzblatt* I, p. 537, part 3, chapter 5, section I, § 15 paragraph 1). The provisions will apply also to officials of social insurance organizations having the status of civil servants.

(3) Civil servants already in retirement are to be considered civil servants for the purposes of this law.

(4) The National Bank (*Reichsbank*) and the German Railways Corporation (*Deutsche Reichsbahn-Gesellschaft*) are empowered to implement parallel regulations.

§ 2

(1) Civil servants who have entered the service since 9 November 1918, without possessing the required or customary educational background or other qualifications for their career track are to be dismissed from service. Their previous salaries will continue to be paid for a period of three months following their dismissal.

(2) They will have no claim to temporary pensions, full pensions or survivors' benefits, nor to retain the rank or titles of office, or to wear service uniforms or emblems

Fig 1a

(3) In case of need and especially if they care for dependents without income, they may be allotted a pension, which can be withdrawn at any time, for up to a third of whatever basic salary they held in their last position; a reinsurance in accordance with social insurance under Reich law is not permitted.

(4) The provisions in paragraphs (2) and (3) shall be applied appropriately to persons of the kind described in paragraph (1) who have already entered retirement prior to the effective date of this law.

§ 3

(1) Civil servants who are not of Aryan descent are to be retired (§ 8 ff.); if they hold honorary posts, they are to be dismissed from their official duties.

(2) Section 1 does not apply to civil servants who were already in office on 1 August 1914 or who fought at the front for the German Reich or its Allies in the World War, or whose fathers or sons fell in the World War. Further exceptions for civil servants working abroad may be permitted by the Reich Minister of the Interior in consultation with the Minister concerned or with the highest state authorities.

§ 4

(1) Civil servants whose previous political activities afford no assurance that they will at all times give their unreserved support to the national state, can be dismissed from the service. They will be allowed to take their earnings for a period of three months following their dismissal. From this point forward they will receive three quarters of the retirement pension (§ 8) and corresponding survivors' benefits.

§ 5

(1) When official need demands it, every civil servant must be prepared to accept transfer to a different appointment having the same or equivalent career track, including positions with a lower rank and service income schedule—with payment of prescribed relocation expenses. In the case of transfer to a position of lower rank and service income schedule the official retains his previous rank designation and the service income of the previous position.

(2) Instead of transfer to a position of lower rank and service income schedule (paragraph 1) the official may within the one month request entry into retirement.

Reich Chancellor
Adolf Hitler

Reich Minister of Interior
Frick

Reich Minister of Finance
Graf Schwerin von Krosigk

Fig 1b

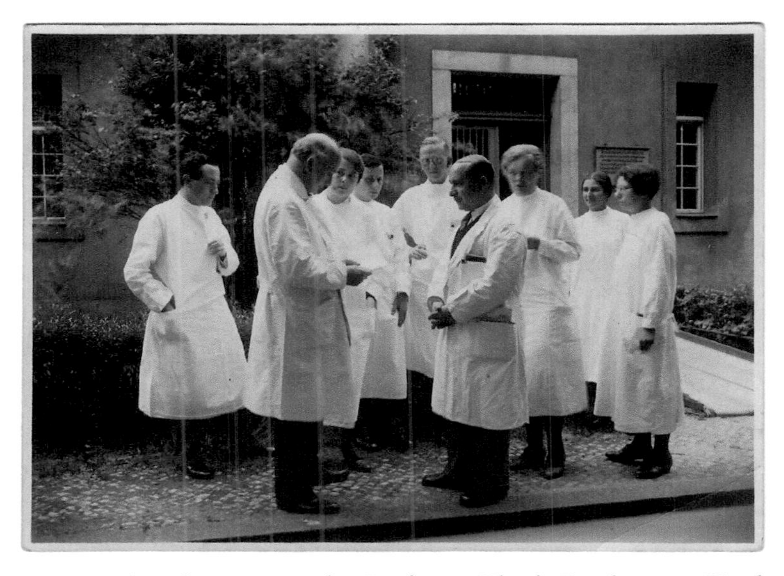

Fig 2 Arthur front row right, Professor Ulrich Friedemann Head of Unit front row left, and colleagues Rudolph-Virchow Hospital.

Susanne Doetz, Christoph Kopke
»und dürfen das Krankenhaus nicht mehr betreten«
Der Ausschluss
jüdischer und politisch unerwünschter
Ärztinnen und Ärzte
aus dem Berliner städtischen Gesundheitswesen
1933–1945
HENTRICH & HENTRICH

Fig 3 “and they (The Jews) will never again be allowed to enter the hospital”

Fig 4

"ST MARY'S HOSPITAL "
ACTION GROUP

Tel: 01.723.1252, ext. 5028.

all correspondence to:
The Secretary
St Mary's Hospital Action Group
St Mary's Hospital
Norfolk Place
London W2 **1NY**

20 December 1988

The Rt. Hon. Kenneth Clarke,
Minister of State for Health,
Department of Health and Social Security,
Richmond House,
Whitehall, London SW1

Dear Mr. Clarke,

Re RAWP and Inner Cities

We understand that the policy of reallocation of resources away from the inner cities is being phased out. This is welcome news because of the reduction in service provision which has already occurred to provide for this policy. The Government has been of some assistance to London in providing interim relief money to compensate for the withdrawal of resources from London.

However, we feel bound to draw your attention to the fact that a regional policy of distributing resources away from London to the periphery of the regions is still in existence. In the North West Thames Region this takes the form of a contribution from our district, Parkside, to their Regional Strategy Development Fund. In the current year this amounts to £1.1m. with a further £1.2m. in 1989/90. We understand that the Government does not wish for any further closure of wards and services. However, if our contribution to the Regional Strategy Development Fund continues at its present level, services in our district may well have to be reduced. Our combined district, Parkside (previously Paddington and North Kensington, and Brent), has produced over £15m. in real terms in the cost improvement programme over the last five years.

We would like to ascertain whether the policy of withdrawing money from inner city areas, and especially teaching districts such as our own, to outer parts of the Region still continues to be Government policy and we would also like to know whether it is based on a sound knowledge of case-mix and indices for deprivation.

If not, we ask for assistance in questioning our Regional Health Authority with regard to the extent of our contribution to its Strategic Development Fund to prevent further contraction of services in this District, and to allow the use of savings achieved by efficiency to be retained locally.

Yours sincerely,

St Mary's Hospital Action Group.

signatures appended.

Copy to Chairman, NW Thames Regional Health Authority.

LETTERS TO THE EDITOR

The real risks of Chernobyl

From Dr Alex Comfort

Sir, It is disconcerting to hear ministers arguing, in the aftermath of Chernobyl, that coalmining and natural gas have a price in accident risk too. They have – but the argument suggests that the arguers do not realize that the nuclear risk differs in kind: radioactive pollution can be irrecoverable.

This is doubly important for Britain. A single severe nuclear power accident could not disable the USA or the USSR – contamination from one Chernobyl-sized accident could under certain conditions make a large part of Britain permanently uninhabitable. No other risk is comparable – the implication is that we cannot afford the possibility.

That our reactor systems are safe or reasonably safe is therefore beside the point. Quite apart from accident, their presence means that a single terrorist, or a single conventional air strike, could remove us from the economic and political map. That successive governments have blandly accepted this situation can only imply a failure of comprehension which is profoundly alarming.

I am, Sir, etc,
ALEX COMFORT,
The Windmill House,
The Hill,
Cranbrook, Kent.

From Professor J. H. Turnbull

Sir, In assessing the hazards presented to this and other countries by the Chernobyl disaster, one should note that this was a *chemical*, not a nuclear explosion. As a result the major products dispersed in the atmosphere would consist of particles of reactor elements disintegrated by

Hospital concern at London cuts

From Dr R. P. H. Thompson and others

Sir, We are consultants working in the health districts of inner London and have been monitoring the deterioration of the hospital services in our area.

These 10 districts are responsible for the care of some two million people and the training of approximately 30 per cent of UK medical graduates. However, during the last five years over £35 million has been cut from our district budgets and this, taken with the shortfall due to health service inflation, has caused the closure of 20 hospitals and more than 2,500 acute medical beds.

We understand a further £90 million, including £25 million of the current allocation of £120 million for the new Riverside district (Fulham, Chelsea and Westminster) alone, and a further 2,500 more beds are to be removed.

It is no exaggeration to say that the care of the sick and the proper training of tomorrow's doctors are now being jeopardised in our hospitals. Already services to the population of London are being curtailed, and many waiting lists are lengthening as the emergency admissions fill the reduced numbers of beds. The inner London population is no longer receiving an adequate acute medical service.

These severe cuts have been imposed by calculations based upon the principle of redistribution of resources on egalitarian lines (Resource Allocation Working Party: RAWP), but the calculations do not allow for different needs in different parts of the country. They have been imposed on a population that is rich only in the socially deprived, the elderly and those having special priorities such as single-parent families, the homeless and those scourged by Aids.

The recent imposition of yellow alerts by the Emergency Bed Service underlines the shortage of facilities, so that the lives of our local people are being made even more miserable, because we can cope only with an increase in acute illness at the expense of waiting lists. The future of hospital medical services in London looks grim, and yet even in your columns there are reports of problems in other regions. The health service has been under-funded for many years and must have more money if it is to provide a modern medical service.

Yours etc,
R. P. H. THOMPSON (St. Thomas' Hospital),
P. K. BARNES (Westminster Hospital),
DESMOND CROFT (St Thomas' Hospital),
R. S. ELKELES (St Mary's Hospital),
ANTHONY HOPKINS (St Bartholomew's Hospital),
R. K. KNIGHT (Guy's Hospital).
ANTHONY PARKINS (Charing Cross Hospital),
ROY POUNDER (Royal Free Hospital),
M. SARNER (University College Hospital),
W. W. SLACK (Middlesex Hospital),
MARK WANSBROUGH-JONES (St George's Hospital),
ROGER WILLIAMS (King's College Hospital),
St Thomas' Hospital, SE1.
May 10.

Doctors dubious

From the President of the Hospital Consultants and Specialists

(ear, nose and throat), psychiatry, radiotherapy and paediatrics are all suffering from this problem, whereas 100 or more doctors

Fig 5

Fig 6

Gastrointestinal Laboratory
The Rayne Institute
St. Thomas' Hospital, London SE1 7EH
Telephone: 071-928 9292 Ext. 3050

Rt Hon William Waldegrave MP
Department of Health
Richmond House
Whitehall
London SW1

3rd December 1990

Dear Mr Waldegrave

I and some of my colleagues representing the twelve London University Hospitals have met over some years now with several Health Secretaryies and Ministers of Health to discuss the increasingly impoverished hospital health services in London. It is therefore with feeling close to despair that I read an account that during a recent parliamentry debate you yourself suggested that the reductions of beds has been balanced by the increase of day surgery. I would like to point out that this year the situation is so bad that I am quite unable to admit patients from my clinics or who are referred to me unless they are literally unable to go home. This means that I see patients who in my clinical judgement, really should be urgently in hospital and I have to put them on a waiting list which means at present that they are unlikely to come into hospital at all. At the same time we know that if a patient is able to pay or is insured, they can be admitted to private hospitals quickly.

I cannot think that this is a situation that you or the Conservative Party can think is right. As I have pointed out to your predecessors I have always believed that the Party was the best one to support the small man and yet he is now made to suffer purely on financial grounds. I therefore beg you not to believe statements and suggestions that hospitals can live within their allocations without seriously damaging the clinical care to the NHS patients and consider ways in which the goverment can improve the now appalling service which we offer to uninsured patients in this city. It may be the situation is equally bad across the country, but I strongly suspect that with the special problems that we have and that we pointed out to your predecessors, that this is a problem particularly bad here in the London.

I am wondering whether it would be possible for you to meet with myself and one or two colleagues to place before you our concern over the local services as we go into the winter.

Yours sincerely

R P H Thompson DM FRCP
Consultant Physician

Copy to: Dr R Elkeles - St Mary's Hospital

FASHION
SERIOUS CASHMERE
CENTRE PAGES

The LONDON STANDA[RD]

Tuesday, May 13, 1986 20p Incorporating the Lo[ndon]

Consultants' warning on London hospitals cash

'HEALTH CUTS CRISIS'

CONSULTANTS from eleven London teaching hospitals claim today that NHS cash cuts for the inner city have been so severe that the care of their patients is now in jeopardy.

The public protest, from some of Britain's most senior doctors, threw the Health Service into the centre of the political arena, just as Mrs Thatcher is under heavy pressure to spend more on key services.

The doctors have been spurred into action by news that one of London's ...

by Alan Massam and Charles Reiss

Guy's, Charing Cross, the Royal Free, University College, the Middlesex, St George's and King's College hospitals.

In all they represent 10 health districts responsible for the care of about two million people and for the training of 30 per cent of UK ...

Fig 7

Fig 8

2—The LONDON STANDARD, THURSDAY, MAY 15, 1986

P.O. to send parcels by road

Standard Reporter

THE Post Office has decided to switch its parcel service from rail to road.

Parcels have been carried by the rail network almost since the inception of the railways 150 years ago.

Now, with the exception of a small volume of parcels to outlying towns, the Post Office will carry all its own parcels by road or air.

British Rail will lose a contract worth £13 million a year and about 400 railway jobs are at risk.

News of the decision was disclosed at Bournemouth by Bert Lyons, secretary of TSSA, the rail white collar union.

He told delegates to his union's conference that the decision was "bleak" and added: "Co-operation between nationalised industries is now non-existent, irrespective of cost."

The amount of remaining parcels traffic was estimtted at less than £1 million.

BR confirmed the Post Office decision and a spokesman said there had been lengthy negotiations over the price and quality of the service.

Medical services 'will be thrown into chaos'

Cash-hit hospital to shut earlier

by Alan Massam

ONE OF north London's key hospitals, St Mary's, Harrow Road, is to close 18 months ahead of schedule.

Although it was decided to close the hospital as soon as possible, October seems the most likely date.

The decision will throw medical services over a wide area into chaos, senior hospital consultant Dr Robert Elkeles warned today.

It was announced last night by Paddington and North Kensington District Health Authority.

Dr Elkeles, head of diabetic services and a member of the health authority, said: "This decision was made with the utmost reluctance and represents the least painful of several options to save about £800,000."

Evils

Alternatives included the closure of wards in St Mary's, Praed Street and St Charles's hospitals.

Services will be absorbed by the expansion of St Mary's, Praed Street. But Dr Elkeles now feared that closing the Harrow Road facilities 18 months earlier than planned would put "enormous extra burdens" on already over-

"But the closure of St Mary's, Harrow Road, really represents the lesser of several evils. Everybody is most unhappy about the decision."

He added: "I really don't know how doctors are going to fit all the patients in. I think we are in for 18 months of chaos."

Last night's meeting of the health authority received about 80 protest letters from local residents and organisations.

The decision will need the approval of the Health Minister.

...lic is that the health ministers take note of the current political climate and reverse this decision," said Mrs Linden.

The closure date was far too short a period to achieve the more efficient management and service which had been sought in the original closure plans, she said.

Closure would mean 110 fewer beds available in the area, said Mrs Linden.

"Inevitably there would be longer waiting lists."

Death

Consultant surgeon Mr ...

Ambulance man Noel Egan, 28, described the decision as senseless.

"We will have to start making decisions about people's lives. If we have someone on board who is dying and Praed Street is full, as it so often is, we will have to choose between St Charles's Hospital, two miles away, or even University College Hospital in Euston.

"It could mean life or death for the patients and we shouldn't be forced to play God."

'The NHS isn't failing'

A LEADING health authority chairman hit back today at doctors who claim London's medical services are failing.

Mr David Berriman, chairman of the North-East Thames Regional Health Authority, says in a letter to The Times that he strongly disputes their conclusions.

"There is a massive change occurring in London. Some of this involves reduction in acute services in the inner city where there has been a major fall in population," he says.

"This region, which is responsible for the hospital and hospital-based services for nearly 4,000,000 residents of North-east London and Essex, with a revenue budget approaching £1,000,000 a year, has made enormous strides in developing its services over the past years, opening major new hospitals in places such as Colchester and Newham and this year the new Homerton Hospital in Hackney."

Mr Berriman says that the number of patients treated has been increasing every year while new day hospitals for the elderly, health centres, drug clinics and community centres have been opened.

"As regional chairman, I have fought and will continue to fight for additional resources," he said. "However, financial resources will always be constrained and the challenge is to use these in the most effective way."

Michael Heath

"Well at least we've got the world's biggest dry dock."

Jobless trend rising

UNEMPLOYMENT rose by 1282 to 3,325,058 in April, Government figures showed today.

The main reason for the increase was a 27,562 rise in the number of unemployed school-leavers looking for work for the first time after Easter.

The rise in unemployed school-leavers to a total of 112,388 outweighed a 26,28[0] fall in adult unemployment during April.

But even the drop in adult jobless was less than the normal seasonal reduction and as a result the underlying jobless trend remained upwards.

Fig 9a

The NHS Review

St. Mary's Hospital, W.2.

A meeting of the consultant staff, St. Mary's Hospital, W2, was held on 30 March 1989 in order to consider the NHS Review and the subsequent Working Papers. About fifty consultants attended and at the conclusion of the meeting they agreed that a small working group should draw up a memorandum setting out the views which had the support of the majority of those who attended the meeting.

MEMORANDUM

The following were welcomed:

1. **The involvement of clinicians in management (the resource management initiative)** provided that clinicians received the necessary management, secretarial and information technology support and provided it was recognised that this would mean taking clinicians away from patients and, in the absence of a significant expansion of the consultant grade, this could mean longer waiting lists.
2. **Cross-boundary payments** so that units are rewarded for the work which they attract rather than being penalised as in the present system.
3. **The ending of RAWP.**
4. **The creation of 100 extra consultant posts** although that amounts to less than one per district.

The following might be accepted given that the details are the subject of negotiation with the medical profession:

1. **Changes in the Distinction Award System.**
2. **Management involvement in consultant appointments.**
3. **Medical audit** which must mean ***clinical audit*** that does not degenerate into a cumbersome administrative exercise in cost-benefit analysis.

There were serious reservations and anxieties about the following:

1. **Self-governing hospitals.**
2. **Possible fragmentation of care.**
3. **Capital charging.**
4. **The philosophy and cost of the 'internal market'.**
5. **The effect of the White Paper on teaching and research.**
6. **The failure to address the problem of chronic underfunding.**

The reasons are set out in the following paragraphs:

a. Self-governing Hospitals

The separation of the district from its hospital may operate to the disadvantage of district patients. There will be two boards of management, with different objectives. The hospital board will have to seek as many lucrative contracts as possible. The district board will seek to care for the local population. The hospital will naturally favour the treatment of those patients who attract more money than those which are a burden such as those with chronic disease e.g. arthritis, diabetes and mental illness. The further separation of hospital and community services seems particularly damaging.

A further concern about self-government was the conflict it might cause within hospitals in which many consultants opposed the scheme. Conflict could also arise between hospitals in the same district if some chose self-government while others did not.

The timetable for self-government was considered unrealistic and there was insufficient information on which to base a rational decision about declaration of interest by the proposed deadline of 8th May 1989.

b. Fragmentation of Care

The institution of the internal market with the district, and some GPs looking for best value for money contracts for groups of patients could lead to fragmentation of patient care. Thus patients with chronic conditions such as breast cancer or diabetes could find themselves attending different hospitals for different aspects of their treatment. This could impede the coordination and increase the inconvenience of their care. This would also have an adverse effect on teaching and research.

c. Capital Charging

The imposition of capital charges could adversely affect inner city hospitals, especially London Teaching Hospitals like St. Mary's. Their sites, through no fault of their own, are extremely valuable. We assume that the

Fig 9b

capital charges to be incurred would be proportionately high. These high costs, coupled with the high costs of employing labour in London, would make it very difficult for these institutions to be financially competitive.

d. The Internal Market: Philosophy and Cost

Philosophy

We do not believe that the market philosophy should be applied to health care, which is a service and not a business. We entirely support the drive for increased efficiency in the NHS. However, with the exception of certain surgical procedures, there is no easily defined product. Competition already exists between institutions in their reputations and ability to attract patients. This should be further encouraged with the use of cross boundary flows of money. There is, however, no need to disturb the present system to achieve this.

Cost

One of the main aims of introducing competition is to contain costs. There is evidence that, contrary to what is intended, costs will escalate.

Experience in the USA has shown that costs rise in the competitive market.[1 & 2] The USA now has the highest ratio of bureaucrats to health care workers in the industrialised world. Between 1980 and 1986 health expenditure in the USA rose by 85%. Administrative costs rose by 186%. Much of this is taken up with the administration of contracts including pricing, monitoring and litigation. Implementation of this type of funding would require a new tier of administrative and accountancy staff. There is also serious doubt as to whether sufficient numbers of the right quality staff are available for this work. With hospitals free to set their own rates of pay there could be an explosion in labour costs.[3]

We conclude that the institution of the internal market will increase costs and in the absence of new money will result in reduction in service.

e. Teaching and Research

The provision of adequate facilities for teaching and research is vital for the future of medicine in this country. These activities cost time and money, which the government recognises. However it is difficult for these activities to flourish in an atmosphere regulated by contracts and treatment at the cheapest possible price. The White Paper gives little guidance on how the quality of teaching and research can be maintained.

The fragmentation produced by some hospitals becoming self-governing will make it difficult to provide an even clinical basis for the training of medical students.

f. Failure to Address the Problem of Chronic Underfunding

There is a consensus among those working in the NHS and many outside that the main problem is chronic underfunding. This conclusion was also reached by the all party Select Committee on Social Services.[4] Britain spends almost the lowest proportion of its GNP on health care of any industrialised nation,[3] yet has an overall health record which is at least as good as that of other countries. Thus the charges of inefficiency and poor value for money are difficult to sustain and further efficiency savings and cost improvements are becoming progressively more difficult. We conclude that a greater level of funding is required.

THE WAY FORWARD

1. **Commitment to a greater level of funding is required. The prime requirement is for capital investment in buildings and equipment and for provision of staff in sufficient numbers and quality, rather than for changes in the accountancy system.**
2. **The government should enter into a constructive dialogue with the profession. Representatives of medical schools should be included, so that effects of change on training and research can be identified. The level of health care which is desirable and which the country can afford needs to be defined. We need evolution and not revolution to modernise the NHS. The profession is not against change. Many changes have already been adopted. Medical audit has gained widespread acceptance. Experiments have been carried out in resource management. Where change is found necessary, it should be based on schemes which have been shown to work.**

   The government should be warned against introducing a radically new system of running the Health Service without knowledge of the ramifications and side-effects of such a system which can only be gained by a preliminary 'pilot trial'.

References

1. Lee, PR, and Etheridge, L 'Clinical freedom: Two lessons for the UK from US experience with privatisation of health care' *Lancet* 1989, 1, 263.
2. Robinson, JC, and Luft, HS 'Competition and the cost of Hospital Care, 1972-1982' *Journal of the American Medical Association* 1987, 257, 3241.
3. Barr, N, Glennerster, H, Le Grand, J 'Working for patients: the right approach?' London School of Economics, February 1989.
4. Social Services Committee, House of Commons, *Resourcing the NHS*, HMSO, 1988.

April 1989

The cash register may drown out the sound of the ambulance

Independent 26.1.89

Robert Elkeles says service, not profit, should be the driving force of the NHS

A year ago, in response to growing concern over scarcity of resources for health care, the Government announced a review of the NHS, which was welcomed by doctors. Publication of the review is due on Tuesday, but parts have been heavily leaked.

It appears that a large input has come from the collective wisdom of three right-wing think-tanks: the Adam Smith Institute, the Centre for Policy Studies and the Institute for Economic Affairs. The common theme is that health care can be bought and sold like merchandise. An organisation called a Health Management Unit (HMU) would buy and sell services for patients and seek "best buys" for these services. Patients might be sent to hospital A for a hip operation, hospital B for obstetrics and hospital C for diabetes treatment. As far as can be judged from information available, the Government proposes to modify the role of district health authorities so that they may act as HMUs without using this name.

I do not believe that medicine can be packaged in this way. Patients frequently have multiple problems; if care is fragmented, we may be in danger of forgetting the patient as a whole. Communication can be difficult even within one institution — between separate hospitals it is likely to be non-existent. The emphasis will be on treatment at the lowest cost rather than achieving the best result.

One of the Government's stated aims is to increase consumer choice. At present, family doctors can refer patients to any hospital they like. The GP may prefer a hospital close to the patient's home or one in which there is particular expertise. Under the proposed arrangements, GPs would hold budgets: their referrals would be dictated by price, so limiting consumer choice.

A system whereby hospitals will be able to opt out of local health authority control is also being put forward. This could tempt some hospitals to concentrate on areas which bring in revenue, such as coronary bypass operations, while discarding other, less profitable ones, such as care of the elderly. Some services might cease to be provided locally. The role of a hospital in providing services to the local community appears to be in question.

The private sector is singled out by the Government for praise. There is a place for private medicine and perhaps this should be expanded, but the Government and the public seem strangely unaware of its shortcomings and lack of standards. The private sector can cope well with routine surgery, but there is no provision for emergency medicine. The recent plane and train disasters have demonstrated the value of emergency medical services, which could not be provided easily on a commercial basis.

The seriously ill patient in a private hospital may be in danger due to the lack of experienced junior staff and to inaccessibility of consultants. The private sector has no body to regulate standards. Doctors who are not consultants, for example, can set themselves up as "specialists" in a field. The only regulatory body appears to be "market forces", — not sufficient to protect the public from inappropriate medical advice.

It should be remembered that all the advances in medicine in this country have come from the NHS and from academic departments within university hospitals. The private sector has not contributed significantly to teaching and research, yet relies heavily on these for its provision of services.

In anticipation of the Government's NHS review there has been an unprecedented attack on consultants. The object is presumably to soften up resistance to forthcoming changes. They have been portrayed as lazy, neglecting their NHS duties for the sake of earning huge sums in private practice, and of awarding each other enormous merit payments on the old-boy network. The reality is different: most consultants work extremely hard for the NHS. Many supplement their income with private practice, but few earn the vast sums often quoted, which usually refer to "A+" awards, limited to a small number of distinguished consultants, probably about 100 in total.

It is true that a minority of consultants abuse the system and fail to carry out their NHS duties. It is to the eternal shame of the profession that such unscrupulous behaviour has not been curbed. However, consultants are human beings and there is no section of society which does not have its share of bad apples. It is a delusion to pretend that this is a major cause of problems in the NHS and an insult to the many who have devoted a lifetime of service to it.

I would have liked the review to begin with a definition of what care is needed in each health region and district. One could then work out how this could be financed. Instead, the trend seems to be to provide a budget and then decide what to spend it on.

A few areas in the health service require special attention. The pay and conditions of physiotherapists, medical records staff, medical secretaries, receptionists, laboratory scientists and many others need careful consideration, so that enough people of the right calibre can be recruited and retained. Lack of support provided by these groups renders the best medical skills ineffective. We need far more good accommodation for the elderly in the community and nursing homes so that the increasing number of elderly patients and those with disability can be cared for in appropriate circumstances — not in acute hospital beds as so often occurs at present.

Proper provision for academic medicine, which has undergone such contraction in recent years, needs to be made so that we can regain our leading position in medical research and train doctors of high quality. The policy recently agreed between the Department of Health and certain representatives of the profession, in which the number of hospital registrar posts is to be radically reduced without alternative provision, should be re-examined before serious damage to service occurs.

Much has already been achieved in making the NHS more cost effective and the Government can rightly claim credit for providing the stimulus for this. Most now agree that room for further cost-efficiency saving is limited.

There is a widespread consensus that the main problem now is underfunding of health care. This was established recently by the House of Commons All Party Social Services Committee. Whether the extra funds come from taxation or from insurance remains to be ascertained. Above all, we should realise that health care is not a business, in which profit is the driving force, but a service.

The author is a consultant physician at St Mary's Hospital, London.

Fig 10

DEPARTMENT OF OBSTETRICS AND GYNAECOLOGY
ST. MARY'S HOSPITAL MEDICAL SCHOOL
LONDON W2 1PG
(01-725 1461)

Professor: R.W. BEARD, MD, FRCOG
Reader: D.B. PAINTIN, MB, ChB, FRCOG
Senior Lecturer: P.J. STEER, MD, BSc, MRCOG
Senior Lecturer in Reproductive Endocrinology: DR. S. FRANKS, MD, MRCP

25th January

My dear Bob,

I greatly enjoyed your article in the Independent and very much hope that it is published. The points that you make about blackening the image of the Consultant by the Government, and the inference of superficial thinking in all proposals for change to date are particularly well taken.

Fig 11a

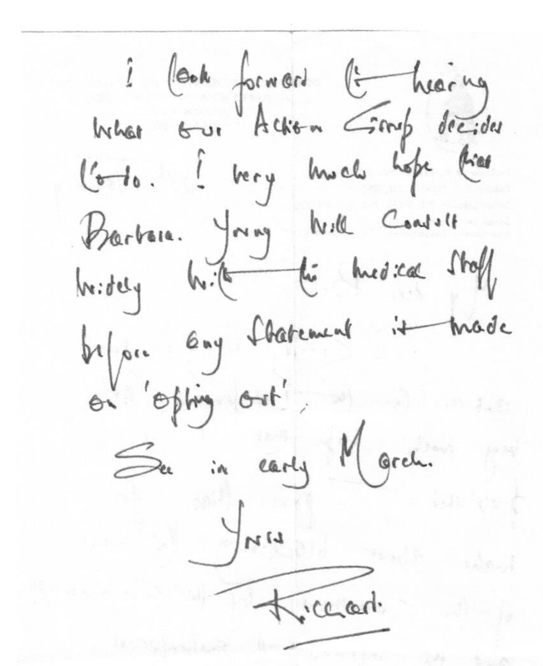

I look forward to hearing what our Action Group decides to do. I very much hope that Barbara Young will consult widely with the medical staff before any statement is made on 'opting out'.

See you in early March.

Yours

Richard

Fig 11b

St Mary's Hospital Medical School

Norfolk Place London W2 1PG 01-723 1252

30 Jan 89

Bob/

That was a super article. I read it with great approval but missed the note at the bottom, thinking that they had excellent editorial staff!

It really is the most important moment since 1948. Can we get the profession together on the primacy of service?. The Colleges are going to have to come in on this, together with BMA. United the docs can beat any govt. when fighting for patients.

With Compliments

Yrs, Peter.

Fig 12

Fig 13

PARKSIDE HEALTH AUTHORITY
Bays 6 & 7, 16 South Wharf Road, London W2 1PF
01-725 [Direct Line]
01-725 6666 [Main Switchboard]

BSY/DFC 1 February 1989

PERSONAL

Dr R Elkeles
St Mary's Hospital
W2

Dear Robert

Your piece in the Independent last week was first class.

I am sure above all that the argument, neatly upstaged over the last few months by the Review, that we simply do not spend enough on health care in this country, should not be forgotten.

Yours sincerely

Barbara

BARBARA S YOUNG
District General Manager

cc Chairman

BMJ April 26 2008.

LETTERS

...he letters for these pages from the rapid ...posted on bmj.com favouring those received ...days of publication of the article to which they ...ters are thus an early selection of rapid responses ...icular topic. Readers should consult the website ...ull list of responses and any authors' replies, which ...arrive after our selection.

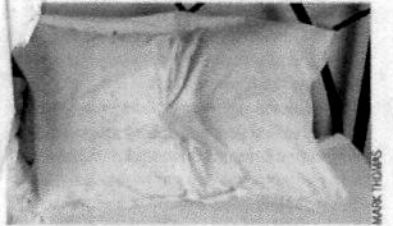

CONTINUOUS DEEP SEDATION

Dutch research reflects problems with the Liverpool care pathway

The Liverpool care pathway (LCP) is the UK's main clinical pathway of continuous deep sedation and is promoted for roll out across the NHS.[1] Rietjens et al's study highlights some serious weaknesses in its design.[2]

The eligibility criteria do not ensure that only people who are about to die are allowed on to the pathway. They allow people who are thought to be dying, are bed bound, and are unable to take tablets on to the pathway. In chronic diseases such as dementia, dying can take years, but such patients may be eligible. Reitjens et al's paper shows that GPs often put patients on to such a pathway without palliative care advice. A pathway for general use should minimise opportunities for early or inappropriate use.

Murray et al are concerned that sedation is being used as an inexpensive alternative to assessment and specialist treatment.[3] The LCP recommends sedatives and opiates for all patients on an "as required" basis, even when they are not agitated, in pain, or distressed. An automatic pathway towards prescribing heavy sedatives incurs risks.

Moreover, the LCP recommends setting up a syringe driver within four hours of a doctor's order. This is laudable, if it is needed. But the pathway encourages the use of syringe drivers even when symptoms can be managed without them.

The pathway doesn't mention the need for food and fluids. Reitjens et al show that withholding artificial nutrition and hydration is the norm. The LCP's omission of prompts to reconsider nutrition and hydration may allow serious errors in the care of dying patients. It is not acceptable, as Murray et al suggest, that assessing nutrition and hydration are not part of the pathway.

Sedation is right in some situations. But as Murray et al point out, the anticipated outcome of continuous deep sedation is death. We must learn from Reitjens et al's observation that continuous deep sedation may replace euthanasia. If the methods and pathways that we use for continuous deep sedation in the UK are flawed, then patients will die as a result of inappropriate use. I hope that the LCP will be reviewed and modified.

Adrian J Treloar consultant and senior lecturer in old age psychiatry, Memorial Hospital, London SE18 3RZ
adrian.treloar@oxleas.nhs.uk

Competing interests: None declared.

1 Marie Curie Palliative Care Institute. *Liverpool care pathway for the dying patient (LCP)*. 2008. www.mcpcil.org.uk/liverpool_care_pathway.
2 Rietjens J, van Delden J, Onwuteaka-Philipsen B, Buiting H, van der Maas P, van der Heide A. Continuous deep sedation for patients nearing death in the Netherlands: descriptive study. *BMJ* 2008;336:810-3. (12 April.)
3 Murray SA, Boyd K, Byock I. Continuous deep sedation in patients nearing death. *BMJ* 2008;336:781-2. (12 April.)

COMPETITION IN THE ENGLISH NHS

Let's return to representative planning for a population

Ham has reached the conclusion that the market approach to health care is not appropriate for disease prevention and chronic disease, and he argues for integration in health care.[1] Most people working in the NHS have thought that the so called market is inappropriate for health care since it was introduced in the 1990s.[2] Competition between health providers is espoused by politicians, journalists, and health economists as the best way to motivate people to work harder and improve efficiency. In fact, the market sets different parts of the NHS against each other and leads to a fragmented approach, rather than ensuring that all work together for the welfare of patients. It sets primary care against secondary care and both types of care against social services. Is this good care?

Ham points to weaknesses in commissioning. It is ridiculous to exclude secondary care specialists from this process. As Ham points out, negotiating contracts in the market is hugely costly. Millions of pounds could be re-directed to patient care, disease prevention, and hospital building by abandoning the market approach and by ridding the NHS of the armies of management consultants.

Let us return to a system where health care is planned for a given population by, for instance, a health authority in which all parts of the NHS are represented. This would ensure an integrated approach and would restore professionalism, pride, and satisfaction in working in the NHS, which have all been reduced by the demeaning market approach. By all means, let health providers compete and be rewarded for providing an excellent and efficient service.

Robert Elkeles consultant physician and professor of diabetic medicine, Imperial College Healthcare NHS Trust, St Mary's Hospital, London W2 1NY
robert.elkeles@kelear.co.uk

Competing interests: None declared.

1 Ham C. Competition and integration in the English National Health Service. *BMJ* 2008;336:805-7. (12 April.)
2 Elkeles R. The cash register may drown out the sound of the ambulance. *Independent* 1989 Jan 26.

SUICIDE AND THE INTERNET

Study misses internet's greater collection of support websites

I'm unsure why Biddle et al's study of suicide and the internet focused on methods of suicide rather than on support, treatment, interventions, crisis hotlines, or information on how to stop or prevent suicide.[1] Suicidal behaviour encompasses all of this and much more.

By stacking the deck with the keywords and search phrases chosen, the researchers found a plethora of websites and information resources on methods of suicide. Their results would probably have been very different had they taken a less biased approach and typed in queries such as "suicide support group", "suicide help", "suicide crisis", or "suicide prevention". When I did a search using "suicide" (the keyword used by most people), the top 10 sites contained no pro-suicide websites.

The researchers made a conscious decision to focus on suicide methods and, as would be expected, found many websites with such information. Even an informational resource might briefly mention such methods to inform and describe what the act of suicide encompasses (but this would not make such a resource a pro-suicide site).

The study was designed to emphasise the negative aspects and did not mention that support websites greatly outnumber pro-suicide websites.

The study paints a pessimistic, biased, and bleak picture of the internet and the suicide resources it offers. Although this picture may true for a small subset of suicidal keywords ...

Fig 14

THE TIMES Tuesday December 1 2009

1 Pennington Street
London E98 1TA

Facsimile 020-7782 5046
E-mail letters@thetimes.co.uk

Effective flood policy and space for water

Sir, The conclusion that flood prevention is much cheaper than flood protection stems from a series of arguments that are scientifically unsound and technically inaccurate (letter, Nov 25). Inland flooding in the UK is caused primarily by the occurrence of rainfall events that are extreme in terms of their prolonged duration and/or their high intensity, falling on ground that is either impermeable or already saturated.

Rises in the incidence of flooding may be explained by increases in both the frequency and magnitude of heavy and prolonged rainfall events, coupled with changes in land use that reduce the ability of rainwater to infiltrate into the ground. While individual floods cannot be directly attributed to climate or land-use change, they are entirely consistent with the expected impacts of global warming and catchment development. Floods like those caused by the huge amount of rainfall experienced in Cumbria cannot be entirely prevented and attempting to do so through river dredging and vegetation clearance would be unsustainable not only in terms of the adverse impacts on habitats and biodiversity, but also in terms of capital costs, repetitive maintenance requirements, aesthetic degradation and social inequality.

The Government recognises that the key to managing flood losses and misery does not lie in the appointment of a "floods czar". It lies in integrated flood risk management (delivered by multiple agencies and stakeholders) that couples "making space for water" through reconnecting rivers to their natural floodplains and wetlands wherever possible, with accurate flood

Politicians of all parties are to blame for failures of NHS

Sir, The rigid pursuit of targets distorts clinical priorities ("Investigation into NHS deaths after hospital scandals", Nov 28, and report, Nov 30). For instance, while the four-hour waiting time for emergency admissions has improved acute care, it has shifted the problems to care thereafter. Patients are often shunted from ward to ward resulting in loss of continuity of care.

The internal market with the purchaser-provider split is wasteful and divisive. The process of negotiating contracts for services in the market is hugely costly. By getting rid of this wasteful market approach, as has been successfully done in Scotland, and also by ridding the NHS of the armies of management consultants, millions of pounds could be redirected to patient care, disease prevention programmes and hospital building.

The market sets different parts of the NHS against each other and leads to a fragmented approach rather than ensuring that all work together for the welfare of patients. A return to a system in which healthcare is planned for a given population would ensure an integrated approach and restore professionalism, pride and satisfaction in working in the NHS, which have all been diminished by the market approach, so inappropriate for healthcare.

The rigid implementation of the European working time directive to 48 hours per week for junior doctors has resulted in doctors who lack sufficient clinical experience and the multiple handovers of patients that adversely affect continuity of patient care. Often the hard-pressed consultants are the only doctors who are familiar with the patients.

Government interference has damaged medical training and performance assessments are made by box ticking rather than properly thought-out references.

The training of nurses also needs to refocus on patient care rather than academic achievement.

Politicians of all parties, guided by wrong-headed academic health advisers, will not admit these problems, preferring to blame managers or health professionals. How many more incidents will happen until they do?

PROFESSOR ROBERT ELKELES
Consultant Physician and
Professor of Diabetic Medicine
Northwood, Middx

Poor old vicars can't do everything

Sir, Of course "the traditional model of a vicar in every parish is over", and for those of us living in rural areas it has been over for 40 years or

full part in the ministry of Christ to the local community. Third, to act as a co-ordinator, making sure, as far as possible, that we had an aim, and

Fig 15

Sacking Nicholson is not the answer for NHS

Sir, Your leader "Hospital Pass" (Mar 1) reaches the wrong conclusion that the NHS is now more efficient with the current financial arrangements. Indeed, it is precisely the business culture encouraged by the internal market and the split between providers and purchasers which is responsible for some of the unsatisfactory attitudes so widely reported.

It has been clear to most working in the NHS that the so-called market has been inappropriate for health care since it was introduced in the 1990s. The idea of competition between health providers plus the purchaser provider split are accepted by most politicians, journalists, health economists and yourselves as the only ways to motivate people in the NHS to work harder and improve efficiency.

In fact it does the opposite. Services are valued only for the income they earn. This leads to the demoralisation and demotivation of staff, especially for those working in areas thought not to be good income generators. Kindness, compassion and dedication cannot be measured and, therefore, cannot be priced like a commodity. It is these qualities which we need to foster by returning to old standards of professionalism.

A return to a planned health care system, as happens in Scotland, would promote an integrated approach to health care and would help to restore professionalism, pride and satisfaction in working in the NHS. It would also help to make the billions of savings now required by eliminating much of the hugely wasteful and complex commissioning process estimated to consume 14 per cent of total NHS costs.

Whether or not Sir David Nicholson remains in post is irrelevant. He is only doing the will of his political masters who fail to understand that healthcare is not a business.

PROFESSOR ROBERT ELKELES
Consultant Physician and Professor of Diabetic Medicine
Northwood, Herts

Sir David Nicholson has faced calls for his resignation as head of the NHS

Sir, The campaign to remove Sir David Nicholson from his role at the top of the NHS is misplaced.

The clinical autonomy of hands-on professionals is highly valued and closely guarded. The concomitant of that autonomy is that the sensitive, humane and competent treatment of individual patients is their responsibility. There is no qualification to this.

It is neither appropriate nor feasible for the chief executive of the entire NHS to be personally accountable for the operational management of an individual hospital, which is where things went so disastrously wrong at Stafford.

If the fundamental challenge of th NHS to live within its means increases the complexity of service provision decisions, the solution is t be found, ideally by consensus, between managers and clinicians or by managerial initiative, within the strategies of a Foundation Trust Board. That board is accountable fo ensuring that standards are appropriate. The NHS Chief Executive is entitled to expect and t demand nothing less.

C. P. VELLENOWETH
NHS Foundation trust clinical governance chairman, 2002-2009
Heswall, Wirral

Sir, Should we now expect Sir David Nicholson to introduce a "compassion target"?

DR ANDREW RIGBY
Tewkesbury, Glos

Fig 16

ay January 8 2015

reet

times.co.uk

Letters to the Ed

sh?

Helping the NHS out of its current crisis

Sir, Your leader "Hospital Pass" (Jan 6) misses one of the main problems affecting our NHS, which is that no politician will admit that the present system of commissioning and procuring services is hugely expensive and wasteful.

Healthcare, just like defence, needs to be planned and not left to market forces. There are good ideas in the NHS England five-year forward view, including the integration of health and social care, but these do not sit comfortably with the business culture which is responsible for some of the unsatisfactory attitudes and behaviour of staff.

Competition between health providers is accepted by most politicians, journalists and health economists as the best way to motivate people in the NHS and improve efficiency. It does not — and is hugely costly.

PROFESSOR ROBERT ELKELES
Northwood, Middx

Sir, Artificial targets that distort clinical priorities have beset the NHS since the Blair government. Instead of treating the sickest patients first, in line with hippocratic principles, staff are diverted to deal with patients whose need may be low or nonexistent,

found that more than a quarter of the public did not know such services existed.

DR EMMA ROWLEY-CONWY
Chairwoman, South East London Doctors on Call

Sir, Katherine Murphy and Mike Smith from the Patients Association (letter, Jan 6) ignore the many out-of-hours GP provider organisations nationally that give good care to patients. They are safe, caring, effective, responsive and well led; not my words, but those of Professor Steve Field of the Care Quality Commission.

DR SIMON ABRAMS
Chairman, Urgent Health UK

Sir, Two ways to help the NHS are to contract all new doctors to work full time for a minimum of five years (this will help staff retention, stop new doctors working abroad straight after qualification, and repay the taxpayers whose money has trained them) and to give A&Es a financial incentive to direct inappropriate patients back to their GP or out-of-hours service.

DR STEPHEN BROWN
Beaconsfield, Bucks

Sir, The flooding of A&Es with unnecessary referrals from NHS 111

have much better levels of health care and most are based on some sort of insurance or payment system. Try saying that and you will be shouted down and told you are evil. So the present shambles will go on, costing more and getting worse. It is the British way.

FRANCIS BOWN
London E3

Sir, While gardening, I got grit in my eye. My surgery said no one could help straight away and booked me to see a doctor. Within five minutes, a doctor rang to say the surgery didn't have "the right equipment" and to go to A&E. A couple of hours later a doctor removed the grit with the "equipment to remove foreign objects in eyes", aka a cotton bud. I saw five NHS staff, all to wield one cotton bud. What a waste of NHS money.

DENNIS CLEMENT
Barnham, W Sussex

Sir, Many of us who rely on the NHS — I have type 1 diabetes — do not enjoy witnessing its politicisation. The service seems to lack long-term strategic planning probably because the political parties tend to plan in blocks of five years or less. Knowing that the bubble caused by the postwar baby boom would have

Defence spendi

Sir, You report the prime mini saying that more defence cuts be ruled out (News, Jan 5). Wi of £1.45 trillion and interest p of £1 billion a week, Whitehall spending cannot continue as i

We need affordable, balanc operationally effective armed to protect the nation and its i There is, however, no room fo cows. Three separate armed f bring unnecessary overheads; sums could be saved with unsentimental reorganisation

LESTER MAY (LT CDR RN, RET
London NW1

Sir, Reports that the prime mi will not ring-fence defence sp will spark concerns of more a redundancies. It is no surpris is struggling to retain person

CATHERINE SPENCER
Chief executive, Army Famili Federation

Sir, This country appears to b spend less than 2 per cent of defence. If the Conservative p the party to be trusted in this are indeed in trouble.

MARK SHORE
High Wycombe, Bucks

Energy enigma

Fig 17

1GM Tuesday May 24 2016 | THE TIMES

itor

Letters to the Editor should be sent to letters@thetimes.co.uk or by post to 1 London Bridge Street, London SE1 9GF

NHS deficit and hospitals 'running on empty'

Sir, Chris Hopson accurately describes the serious shortfall in NHS funding ("Our health service is running on empty", Opinion, May 21). In addition, large sums are haemorrhaging from the NHS through the present complex system of commissioning healthcare.

The whole process of negotiating contracts for services in the so-called internal market has been estimated to consume 14 per cent of the total NHS budget. This was made worse by Andrew Lansley's Health and Social Care Act, itself estimated to have cost up to £3 billion, which further increased the requirement for competitive tendering. The changes were supposed to reduce bureaucracy but the opposite has happened. GPs on the 211 clinical commissioning groups struggle to combine their work with their commissioning roles. There is an obsession with process rather than on the actual care provided.

The NHS Five Year Forward View offers a possible way of reducing the complexity of commissioning by bringing together primary and acute care (and potentially social care) for a given population. By encouraging closer working together of these health professionals it may be possible to keep more people at home rather than ending up in hospital A&E departments.

The serious shortages of nurses, GPs, and of hospital doctors need to be addressed by effective workforce planning, which has so far been sadly lacking. Many doctors in training are leaving to work abroad to seek better conditions and others are retiring early to escape from the "blame culture" so prevalent in the NHS.

Restoring professionalism and pride in working in the NHS would reduce staff shortages and the need for expensive agency staff. We should stop blaming clinicians and managers for the shortcomings of the system.

PROFESSOR ROBERT ELKELES
Northwood, Middx

Sir, Chris Hopson correctly points out that the current parlous state of the NHS is a systemic problem and not one due to poor leadership on a local level. However, his suggestion that neighbouring A&E departments should be merged sits uneasily with his own observation that the department at Norwich is struggling to cater for twice as many patients as it was designed for. We may be able to cram all the staff from two departments into one, but the remaining one needs to have the physical capacity to cope. I disagree in any case that this will work: history tells us otherwise. The merger of three hospitals into one trust in south London, with the loss of one A&E department, not only failed to save any money but was followed by the first official bankruptcy in NHS history. Likewise, the merger of Hastings and Eastbourne hospitals, while clinically acceptable, has not resulted in any meaningful cost saving. Every acute trust in Kent and Sussex is in special measures, largely because of the inability to reconcile maintaining both good clinical services and financial balance.

It is clear that something is very rotten in the state of the NHS. If the state cannot find more money, we must examine all other funding options, including patient payments.

DR ANDREW BAMJI
Rye, E Sussex

Sir, You report (May 21) that hospitals have racked up an overspend of £2.45 billion. The main unfunded public sector employee pensions are currently costing some £30 billion a year, and rising. The long-term liabilities of these pensions form a substantial component of our national debt. If we were to put these pensions on the same terms as private sector (money purchase) pensions, it would release billions of pounds of taxpayers' money — more than covering the NHS overspend.

BILL PARISH
Bromley, Kent

Par for the course

Sir, Your correspondents have shown a remarkable lack of knowledge of golf in Scotland and Muirfield in particular. As recently as 2013 at Muirfield the R&A's Peter Dawson was reminding the world that "there are six members golf clubs in St Andrews, three all-male and three all-female, and all six clubs are very happy with that arrangement". The only thing that has changed since then is that one of them, the R&A, has bowed to commercial and media pressure to have women members.

There are many other single-sex clubs of both genders throughout Scotland and they are not contemplating change. This is the way that Scottish golf works and will probably continue to do so for the foreseeable future. It works for everyone, especially the ladies, who often enjoy their golf at a fraction of the cost of the men, and this does more to encourage and improve female participation in golf than all the media, political and equality posturing put together.

CHARLES HERD
Gullane, East Lothian

Sir, Leaving the Open golf course roster is surely not the most compelling sanction that may apply to Muirfield. Some years ago my own course, which has full lady members, had a men's bar and a mixed lounge. It was made quite clear to the club by the local authorities that perpetuating

Fig 18

A review into restoring pride in the NHS

Sir, Paul Johnson is correct to point out that we need to ask how the NHS can change for the better and to improve the way in which money is spent ("The NHS doesn't deserve our hero worship", Comment, Aug 25).

Nine out ten hospital trusts are in financial deficit because of increased staffing costs. There is a shortage of nurses and so they have to employ more staff (often from agencies) to comply with safety standards.

There is also a shortage of junior doctors, resulting in consultants having to act down to fill the gaps. Many doctors in training are leaving to work abroad to seek better conditions. GPs are retiring early to escape the relentless pressure and bureaucracy.

We need to retain our workforce by improving working conditions. We need to end the constant tide of blame which is heaped on those trying to provide a service.

The NHS is being asked to find £22 billion in efficiency savings while huge sums are being wasted through the present complex system of commissioning healthcare. By getting rid of this wasteful market approach, as in Scotland, and by ridding the NHS of the armies of management consultants, millions could be redirected to improve standards in primary and social care, disease prevention and hospital building.

The market sets different parts of the NHS against one another and leads to a fragmented approach rather than ensuring that all work together for the welfare of patients.

A return to a system in which healthcare is planned for a given population would ensure an integrated approach, improve care, restore professionalism, pride and satisfaction in working in the NHS.

PROFESSOR ROBERT ELKELES
Northwood, Middx

Sir, Paul Johnson's realistic appraisal of the NHS needs to be understood in Westminster. The NHS has become a political football, with the government claiming how wonderful it is and the opposition putting all its failings down to the government.

The truth is that NHS England is too big to manage even if it did not have the politicians, nearly 2,000 civil servants, 29 quangos and assorted lobby groups. Given all that, it is amazing the NHS is as good as it is.

Norman Lamb, the Liberal Democrat shadow health minister, has called for a cross-party NHS strategic review. Lord Saatchi has, similarly, called for a royal commission. Mr Lamb's petition rapidly gained 83,000 supporters before the last election closed it down. The NHS has always been a vote loser for the Conservatives. Surely they should recognise the benefits to them, as well as the UK, of taking it out of politics?

TIM AMBLER
Cley next the Sea, Norfolk

Sir, On healthcare Paul Johnson says that "we spend a perfectly respectable amount: somewhat less than the French, Germans and Dutch, rather more than the Spanish and Italians".

In fact the French, Germans and Dutch spend about 11 per cent of their GDP on healthcare against our 9 per cent.

However, the GDP per capita of Germany and the Netherlands is significantly higher than ours — about $42,000 and $45,000 respectively against our $40,000 — so their spending on healthcare turns out to be more like 25 per cent more than ours.

GIL PATRICK
Bodmin, Cornwall

Fig 19

Fig 20

Cardiovascular Outcomes in Type 2 Diabetes

A double-blind placebo-controlled study of bezafibrate: the St. Mary's, Ealing, Northwick Park Diabetes Cardiovascular Disease Prevention (SENDCAP) Study

ROBERT S. ELKELES, MD
JUDITH R. DIAMOND, BSC
CLARE POULTER, SRN
SURINDER DHANJIL, MSC
ANDREW N. NICOLAIDES, MS
SHAHID MAHMOOD, MRCP
WILLIAM RICHMOND, PHD
HUGH MATHER, MD
PATRICK SHARP, MD
MICHAEL D. FEHER, MD
THE SENDCAP STUDY GROUP

OBJECTIVE — To determine whether serum lipid intervention, in addition to conventional diabetes treatment, could alter cardiovascular outcomes in type 2 diabetes.

RESEARCH DESIGN AND METHODS — There were 164 type 2 diabetic subjects (117 men, 47 women) without a history of clinical cardiovascular disease randomized to receive either bezafibrate or placebo daily on a double-blind basis in addition to routine diabetes treatment and followed prospectively for a minimum of 3 years. Serial biochemical and noninvasive vascular assessments, carotid and femoral artery B-mode ultrasound measurements, and those pertaining to coronary heart disease (CHD)—clinical history, the World Health Organization (WHO) cardiovascular questionnaire, and resting and exercise electrocardiogram (ECG)—were recorded.

RESULTS — Bezafibrate treatment was associated with significantly greater reductions over 3 years in median serum triglyceride (−32 vs. 4%, $P = 0.001$), total cholesterol (−7 vs. −0.3%, $P = 0.004$), and total-to-HDL cholesterol ratio (−12 vs. −0.0%, $P = 0.001$), and an increase in HDL cholesterol (6 vs. −2%, $P = 0.02$) as compared with placebo. There was a trend toward a greater reduction of fibrinogen (−18 vs. −6%, $P = 0.08$) at 3 years. No significant differences between the two groups were found in the progress of ultrasonically measured arterial disease. In those treated with bezafibrate, there was a significant reduction ($P = 0.01$, log-rank test) in the combined incidence of Minnesota-coded probable ischemic change on the resting ECG and of documented myocardial infarction.

CONCLUSIONS — Improving dyslipidemia in type 2 diabetic subjects had no effect on the progress of ultrasonically measured arterial disease, although the lower rate of "definite CHD events" in the treated group suggests that this might result in a reduction in the incidence of coronary heart disease.

Cardiovascular disease, particularly coronary heart disease (CHD), is the most important cause of morbidity and mortality in type 2 diabetes in Western society. For men with type 2 diabetes, mortality from CHD is two to four times higher than in nondiabetic men, and the corresponding increase is even greater for women (1).

In the general population, increased incidence of CHD is associated with raised serum cholesterol, while there is an inverse relationship with HDL cholesterol. The evidence that elevated serum triglyceride levels is an independent risk factor for CHD in the general population (2,3) is even stronger in the diabetic population (4–6). A raised serum triglyceride level and low HDL cholesterol are characteristic abnormalities in type 2 diabetes. There is much evidence that these two related abnormalities, often referred to as dyslipidemia, are important in the etiology of the accelerated vascular disease in type 2 diabetes (4–6). Fibrinogen elevation has been shown to be an independent risk factor for cardiovascular disease in the general population (7) and also seems to be important in diabetes (8).

Primary prevention studies in middle-aged men with hyperlipidemia, without known CHD, have shown that the incidence of CHD can be reduced by modification of serum lipid concentrations (9–11), but there are as yet no comparable studies specifically in type 2 diabetic subjects. Conventional diabetes therapy has, as yet, not been shown to reduce the incidence of cardiovascular disease (1). Because subjects with type 2 diabetes are a group at high risk for cardiovascular disease, there is a clear need for a prospective study to ascertain whether its progress can be modified. It seems logical to prevent progression of cardiovascular disease by correcting the metabolic abnormalities that are thought to contribute to it, namely by lowering serum triglyceride and cholesterol, raising HDL cholesterol, and lowering fibrinogen. The fibrate drugs provide a means of correcting these abnormalities. Bezafibrate has been shown to decrease serum triglyceride and cholesterol and raise HDL cholesterol over 3 months in type 2 diabetic subjects and to have a small glucose-lowering effect (6,12). In addition, it has also been shown to lower fibrinogen (13).

From the St. Mary's Hospital and Imperial College School of Medicine at St. Mary's (R.S.E., J.R.D., C.P., S.D., A.N.N., S.M., W.R.), London; Ealing Hospital (H.M.), London; Northwick Park Hospital (P.S.), Harrow, Middlesex; and the Department of Therapeutics (M.D.F.), Charing Cross and Westminster Hospital Medical School, London, U.K.

Address correspondence and reprint requests to R.S. Elkeles, MD, Unit for Metabolic Medicine, St. Mary's Hospital, Praed Street, London, W2 1NY, U.K.

Received for publication 10 September 1997 and accepted in revised form 7 January 1998.

Abbreviations: AUS, arterial ultrasound score; CHD, coronary heart disease; ECG, electrocardiogram; IMT, intima media thickness; MI, myocardial infarction; WHO, World Health Organization.

Fig 21

Fig 22

The risks of giving statins to all

Sir, Your headline on July 24 read that "taking statins may increase cancer risk". On July 28 you report that the Government's national director for heart and stroke said that all men over 50 and women over 60 should be offered statins.

What are people supposed to make of all this? There are complex issues behind these stories that need careful scrutiny. In the case of statins it cannot make sense to turn all men over 50 and women over 60 into patients. Treating large numbers of those at very low risk from disease could well uncover hidden side-effects and could detract from the great benefits of these life-saving drugs. It is surely more sensible to give them to who are genuinely at most risk.

We need a more balanced approach to these issues if the public is to retain any confidence in modern medicine.

ROBERT ELKELES
Consultant Physician
St Mary's Hospital, Paddington

Sir, The proposal for cholesterol-lowering statins to be offered to all men over the age of 50 and women over 60 may well have benefits by saving lives, NHS funding and doctors' time.

There will, however, be one unwelcome and potentially costly side-effect for those taking statins as a preventative measure, even where there are no symptons. Quite bizarrely, it is the currrent practice of travel insurance companies either to load premiums or offer no insurance at all to those travellers who take medication for high blood pressure or high cholesterol, even where the medication produces readings which are within government guidelines. The situation is especially acute for those who have reached the age of 65 and wish to travel outside Europe.

What the insurance companies do not seem willing to take into account is that a person on medication that works satisfactorily is a much lower risk than someone they don't know about who might have high blood pressure or cholesterol levels.

COLIN O'KEEFFE
Cosham, Hants

Sir, Late in 1999 I was found to have an ominously high cholesterol count of 270mg/dl. Apart from switching from whole milk to semi-skimmed milk, as recommended by my physician, the only other remedial action I took was to introduce two to three teaspoons of oat bran into my daily diet. Within three months my cholesterol level dropped by 10 per cent to 243, by August 2000 it had sunk to 220, and on 28.6.2001 it recorded a low of only 176 mg/dl.

In view of the known and possibly still unknown side-effects of statins, I am surprised at the proposal to prescribe them to millions of Britons when a cheaper and more natural remedy is readily to hand.

DENNIS B. STUART
Brighton

Join the debate online today timesonline

Junior doctors

● It's astonishing that those responsible for this disaster are still employed, let alone unsanctioned. The amount of time taken away from patient care is huge.
James Taylor, Aberdeen

Tesco jails

● The only punishment for young offenders is one that involves boredom. No teenage hero can brag to his or her friend how he boldly stared at a blank wall for four hours.
John Carty, Medellin, Colombia

Fig 23

Statins success

Sir, Dr Andrew Bamji's unfortunate and misleading comments on statins (letter, May 14) cannot remain unchallenged. There is a very large body of evidence from well-conducted clinical trials that show that statins reduce the incidence of cardiovascular events and mortality in those at increased risk. This risk reduction is clearly related to the observed reductions in blood cholesterol. How that risk is assessed is a different question.

Statins, used correctly, remain one of the true advances in modern medicine.

PROFESSOR ROBERT ELKELES
Northwood, Middx

Corrections and clarifications

The Times takes complaints about editorial content seriously. We are committed to abiding by the Independent Press Standards Organisation ("IPSO") rules and regulations and the Editors' Code of Practice that IPSO enforces. Requests for corrections or clarifications should be sent by email to feedback@thetimes.co.uk or by post to Feedback, The Times, 1 London Bridge Street, London SE1 9GF

children out of school during term time. The costs of a holiday abroad spirals the moment schools break up.

However there is a consequence of taking one's child out of school — lessons missed. Lessons are important, as anyone whose child has guidelines on taki school can be writ understandable, re enforceable.

CHRIS MULLER
Head, Sir William
Chertsey, Surrey

1914 THE FIRST WORLD WAR 1918

ON THIS DAY MAY 16, 1916

THE WOMAN'S BURDEN

That women of the middle classes will have to bear the burden of compulsion is very evident. Military service has introduced comparative comfort into many poor homes, but it will bring comparative poverty to many well-to-do ones. Keeping up appearances will be frankly impossible, and with prices at their present high standard the separation allowance, even with the most generous system of grants to meet rent, mortgage in school fees, insura payments in insta furniture, will be to women whose difficult to meet t £400 or £500 a ye

There has been the middle classes the married wom work after marria interpreted as a sl earning capacity Now that many w been wage-earner must resume work the employment must cease.

As yet at the bu exchanges there h great accession of looking for jobs. T making arrangem homes, which will up, and trying to fi quarters. Premium for small flats and many women are endeavouring to fi into smaller quart

Fig 24

European Heart Journal (2008) 29, 2244–2251
doi:10.1093/eurheartj/ehn279

CLINICAL RESEARCH
Imaging

Coronary calcium measurement improves prediction of cardiovascular events in asymptomatic patients with type 2 diabetes: the PREDICT study

Robert S. Elkeles[1,2*], Ian F. Godsland[1], Michael D. Feher[3], Michael B. Rubens[4], Michael Roughton[5], Fiona Nugara[6], Steve E. Humphries[7], William Richmond[2], and Marcus D. Flather[5,6], for the PREDICT Study Group

[1]Endocrinology and Metabolic Medicine, Imperial College London, St Mary's Hospital, Praed Street, London W2 1NY, UK; [2]Imperial College NHS Trust, London, UK; [3]Beta Cell Unit, Chelsea and Westminster Hospital, London, UK; [4]CT Scanning Unit, Royal Brompton Hospital, London, UK; [5]National Heart and Lung Institute, Imperial College London, London, UK; [6]Clinical Trials and Evaluation Unit, Royal Brompton Hospital, London, UK; and [7]The Rayne Institute, Royal Free and University College Medical School, London, UK

Received 21 January 2008; accepted 5 June 2008; online publish-ahead-of-print 23 June 2008

See page 2193 for the editorial comment on this article (doi:10.1093/eurheartj/ehn368)

Aims The PREDICT Study is a prospective cohort study designed to evaluate coronary artery calcification score (CACS) as a predictor of cardiovascular events in type 2 diabetes (T2DM).

Methods and results A total of 589 patients with no history of cardiovascular disease and with established T2DM had CACS measured, as well as risk factors, including plasma lipoprotein, apolipoprotein, homocysteine and C-reactive protein concentrations, homeostasis model assessment insulin resistance (HOMA-IR), and urine albumin creatinine ratio. Participants were followed for a median of 4 years and first coronary heart disease (CHD) and stroke events were identified as primary endpoints. There were 66 first cardiovascular events (including 10 strokes). CACS was a highly significant, independent predictor of events ($P < 0.001$), with a doubling in CACS being associated with a 32% increase in risk of events (29% after adjustment). Hazard ratios relative to CACS in the range 0–10 Agatston units (AU) were: CACS 11–100 AU, 5.4 ($P = 0.02$); 101–400 AU 10.5 ($P = 0.001$); 401–1000 AU, 11.9 ($P = 0.001$), and >1000 AU, 19.8 ($P < 0.001$). Only HOMA-IR predicted primary endpoints independently of CACS ($P = 0.01$). The areas under the receiver operator characteristic curve for United Kingdom Prospective Diabetes Study (UKPDS) risk engine primary endpoint risk and for UKPDS risk plus CACS were 0.63 and 0.73, respectively ($P = 0.03$).

Conclusion Measurement of CACS is a powerful predictor of cardiovascular events in asymptomatic patients with T2DM and can further enhance prediction provided by established risk models.

Keywords Coronary calcification • Type 2 diabetes • Coronary events • Stroke

Cardiovascular disease (CVD), especially coronary heart disease (CHD), is the most common complication and the principal cause of death in type 2 diabetes (T2DM). The risk of CHD is 2–5 times greater in patients with T2DM than in those free of the disease[1] and there is evidence that its incidence can be reduced by control of hyperglycaemia, hypertension, and dyslipidaemia.[2] Methods are established for assignment of individual risk based on the major risk factors: age, gender, family history, smoking history, blood pressure, diabetes, and lipid profile.[3,4]

Diabetes is now considered a CHD equivalent and patients with T2DM are offered cardiovascular risk reduction. There may, nevertheless, be undetected subgroups at relatively low risk that should not be over-treated, while others may be at high risk and in need of more intensive risk modification. Furthermore, despite

* Corresponding author. Tel: +44 20 7886 1209, Fax: +44 20 7886 1790, Email: robert.elkeles@imperial.nhs.uk

Fig 25

Attitudes of consultant physicians to the Calman proposals: a questionnaire survey

Hugh M Mather, Robert S Elkeles on behalf of the North West Thames Diabetes and Endocrinology Specialist Group

Abstract

***Objective*—To determine the views of a large and representative group of consultant physicians on the Calman proposals, in which acute general medical services will change from being primarily consultant led to consultant provided.**

***Design*—Postal questionnaires.**

***Subjects*—All 236 consultant physicians in acute hospitals in North West and South West Thames regions.**

***Results*—Replies were received from 179 (76%). One hundred and thirty seven (77%) indicated that they would not resume emergency residential duties, and 126 (71%) indicated that they would probably withdraw from general medical duties under these circumstances. One hundred and twenty six (70%) and 137 (77%) had not inserted a central venous line or temporary pacemaker, respectively, within the previous five years. Of 157 answering a question on the impact of the Calman proposals on the quality of patient services, 125 considered that it would be detrimental, and only 18 (11%) thought that it would be beneficial.**

***Conclusion*—Most consultant physicians are not prepared to resume emergency duties and could not do so without retraining in practical procedures. There is widespread antagonism to the Calman proposals, and most physicians consider that their impact on the quality of patient services will be detrimental.**

Ealing Hospital, Southall, Middlesex UB1 3HW
Hugh M Mather, *consultant physician*

St Mary's Hospital, London W2 1NY
Robert S Elkeles, *consultant physician*

Correspondence to: Dr Mather.

BMJ 1995;311:1060-2

Introduction

The Calman report proposes radical changes to the training of junior medical staff that will fundamentally alter the delivery of acute hospital services from being primarily consultant led to consultant provided.[1 2] A reduction in middle grade junior staff will be accompanied by an increase in the number of consultants, who will participate directly in emergency care. These changes have been made explicit in a recent paper from the Committee of Postgraduate Medical Deans (COPMED) and the United Kingdom Conference of Postgraduate Deans, which states that "involvement of the consultants in the provision of emergency care will need to be extended and formalised into their job plans."[3]

The impact on consultants in acute specialities will be profound,[4] especially for physicians in acute general medicine, because of the need for 24 hour cover. Yet there has been surprisingly little reaction from consultant physicians themselves. The Royal College of Physicians and the BMA have both given qualified support to the proposals but have made no attempt to ascertain the views of those colleagues who are most directly affected. We therefore sent a questionnaire on behalf of the North West Thames Diabetes and Endocrinology Specialist Group to a large and representative group of consultant physicians to elicit their views on these issues.

Subjects and methods

A confidential questionnaire was sent in March 1995 to all 236 consultant physicians in North West Thames and South West Thames regions whose junior staff participated in emergency intake duties. They worked at five teaching hospitals and 25 district general hospitals. We received 179 (76%) replies, and the response rates from teaching hospital and district general hospital consultants were 82% (54/66) and 74% (125/170) respectively. The respondents comprised 154 men and 25 women, and their median age was 45-50 years. The largest speciality groups were diabetes/endocrinology (35), geriatrics (34), gastroenterology (29), respiratory medicine (27), and cardiology (22).

CHAPTER 11

Research

At Northwick Park and Clinical Research Centre, although I was reasonably productive, I found it difficult to think creatively about research because it was expected. Ironically, once I got to St Mary's, where there was little expectation that NHS consultants would do meaningful research, I found that I was really keen to contribute. My interest was in the relationship between diabetes and its main complication, that of atherosclerosis (hardening and narrowing of the arteries). I wondered whether the blood fat (lipid) composition was abnormal in people with diabetes and whether such abnormalities could contribute to the increased incidence of arterial disease in diabetes. There was a big metabolic unit in a building called the Mint Wing (Fig 20). This building was originally a stable for horses (The Mint stables), built in the late nineteenth century and used by British Rail, which carried goods arriving at Paddington Station. The man in charge was Professor Victor Wynn. He had come to St Mary's from Australia in 1950. He himself was a man made very wealthy by the family wine business. He persuaded British Rail to sell the building and, with some money from the university, the Nuffield Foundation and a construction company, it was bought for St Mary's. The building was converted into laboratories and a metabolic day ward. Victor Wynn had a reputation for being unpleasant and difficult. Nevertheless, he had the facilities which I needed. Colleagues told me that I would never be able to work with him. Despite these warnings I thought that I would try. I raised money for a technician to work in the lab on high-density lipoproteins. These were part of the fat particles in the blood which were thought to protect against atherosclerosis. His name was Sohail Khan. He was a delightful young man of Pakistani origin. He was easy-going and good-natured. We accordingly did some work and managed to publish two papers, with Victor Wynn named as a co-author. Sometime later he called into his office and accused Sohail of 'destroying his department'. This was quite ridiculous. Sohail was a harmless man who would never have done anything like this. I was furious and came as close as I ever came to hitting anyone. Happily, I did not, but walked out and decided not to work in his department again.

So what to do? By chance there was a scientist working in the department of chemical pathology called Bill Richmond. We had met previously when we were both at Northwick Park. He was a distinguished man who had invented and patented the method which was used worldwide to measure blood cholesterol. We decided to work together. We found a small lab in another part of the Mint Wing and were also able to use the chemical pathology lab. In those days it was much easier to find money for research than it is today. Pharmaceutical companies were often ready to give money to fund a technician or research fellow. Furthermore, the regulatory control on research was much less rigorous than it is today. I was able to fund a series of clinical research fellows and scientists. My first clinical fellow was Susan Rendel. She worked on a new oral hypoglycaemic drug (a drug to lower blood glucose in diabetes). She did not stay long as her husband was a prospective Liberal parliamentary candidate and they moved to the West Country. My next fellow was Paul Seviour. We worked on the way the body handled a fat load given intravenously. We found that young smokers handled the fat load less efficiently than non-smokers. We also found that there were differences in the blood lipid levels in Type 2 diabetic subjects with and without arterial disease. We also found for the first time that a drug called bezafibrate was able to correct these abnormalities. We suggested that this might be a way to prevent arterial disease in Type 2 diabetes. This was published in the journal *Diabetic Medicine*. The editor for some reason insisted on putting it in the clinical audit section when it was in fact original research. Paul went on to a career in general practice in Somerset.

Next came Simon Rains. He investigated the effect of oral hypoglycaemic agents on blood lipid levels. He showed that the important drug metformin lowered blood cholesterol in people with Type 2 diabetes. We were joined by Michael Feher, who worked jointly between me and Professor Peter Sever, professor of clinical pharmacology. He investigated the effects of blood pressure-lowering drugs on blood lipids in people with Type 2 diabetes. Michael went on to become a consultant at Chelsea and Westminster Hospital and has remained a close friend. One of the pleasures of our research was to attend conferences, often held in the beautiful cities of Northern Italy like Padua and Florence. A tradition of our group was to gather in the evening on one of the large squares. To the amusement of passers-by, we raced each other across the square. I was usually last. Simon Rains and Bill Richmond usually won. We called this "the Morgagni Sprint", after Giovanni Morgagni, the Italian anatomist and the father of modern anatomical pathology, who taught at the University of Padua. I remember another occasion when the conference put on an evening of baroque chamber music at an exquisite Italian villa. Such events would not occur today.

On the 9th September 2001, I went to New York to attend a lipid conference with Michael Feher and Bill Richmond. The conference was at the Hilton Hotel. I had never even been to the USA. We all went to the Empire State Building. On Monday evening I was walking in the bustling streets with Michael, who knew New York well. I looked up at the skyscrapers and asked, "What do they do if they have a fire up there?" On Tuesday the 11th, the programme looked as if the afternoon could be missed. I thought that I would use the time to visit the World Trade Centre (WTC). During the morning session I went into the gents' and met a colleague from London, who asked if I had heard that a plane had hit a building. When I got out the dramatic news unfolded of the deadly attack on the WTC and the other atrocities. Happily for me, I did not get to the WTC and realised that I had had a very lucky escape. At the Hilton we were not close to the WTC. From being a bustling city, New York was shut down and deserted. The conference continued, as there was nowhere else for people to go. The following day an appeal for medical help was made on the conference screens. Three of us from London went to a huge hospital to offer our services. This hospital made St Mary's look like a cottage hospital. Our services were not needed. All the phone networks were either shut down or overloaded. I could not contact Arran to tell her that I was safe. She had been at work when the news of this attack emerged. She was unable to contact me and was of course very worried as she knew that I liked to explore. Eventually we were able to make contact, much to her relief. Although travel in and out of New York was heavily restricted, the pharmaceutical company which had sponsored us amazingly managed to get us on a flight only twenty-four hours later.

I also started to work with the department of vascular surgery under Professor Andrew Nicolaides, who was using ultrasound to measure the thickness of the carotid arterial wall (intima media thickness). Another fellow, Peter Merrin, studied and found a relationship between blood cholesterol and intima media thickness in people with Type 1 diabetes. Peter went on to carry out some other good work. His marriage had failed but he then met and later married our senior diabetes sister, Mary Rose Bourke. He ended up in general practice in Truro.

Christopher Baynes had been our clinical registrar. He wanted to do research with our group. We applied for and were awarded a fellowship for him by the Wellcome Trust. This was a prestigious award. Chris carried out some really exciting research. In Type 2 diabetes, resistance to the action of insulin is an important feature of the disease. Chris investigated the relation of insulin resistance in Type 2 diabetes to various metabolic parameters using a sophisticated and difficult tool in which glucose and insulin were infused into patients to achieve a so-called steady state. Chris made a number of interesting observations and published important papers. He went on to become our senior registrar and then consultant at Chase Farm

Hospital. At the same time, I had found money for a lab scientist to work with Bill Richmond and me. We were interested in an enzyme called hepatic lipase produced in the liver. Our scientist, Alec Henderson, developed a method of measuring this enzyme. He found that its activity was related to some of the abnormal blood lipid concentrations in Type 2 diabetes. He studied the control of the synthesis of this enzyme in cultured liver cells. His novel theory to explain the regulation of the enzyme by the cholesterol content within liver cells was rewarded in 1993 by the award of the Fournier Prize for the Young Investigator of the Year by the British Hyperlipidaemia Association. He also provided the biochemical expertise for several of our projects. In December 1993, after giving a presentation to the British Diabetic Association, he reported neurological symptoms. It turned out that he had an advanced brain tumour and died in April 1994. We all felt his loss greatly. We replaced him first with Louise Nimmo and later Avril McColl. I found money for another registrar, Chantal Kong, to join the research team. She studied the relationships between insulin resistance, the enzyme hepatic lipase and the lipid abnormalities in Type 2 diabetes and the ultrasonically measured carotid artery wall thickness. She also found that Type 2 diabetic subjects who smoked had higher enzyme activity, more abnormal blood lipids and increased carotid arterial wall thickness. Chantal went on to become a consultant at Watford General Hospital.

My underlying interest was to find a way of preventing arterial disease in people with Type 2 diabetes, which was the main cause of their increased mortality. We had shown that the drug bezafibrate could improve the blood lipid profile in people with Type 2 diabetes. This was of course before the statin drugs were in widespread use. I considered setting up a study to see whether the drug could reduce mortality in Type 2 diabetes. This, of course, would have been a huge undertaking. I had lunch one day, as was possible then, in the consultants' dining room in the medical school with Professor Geoffrey Rose. He was the founder of cardiovascular epidemiology, a hugely respected figure as well as an incredibly modest man. I believe that he actually went out with Margaret Thatcher when they were both at Oxford. I explained to him what I wanted to do. He warned me off an event-based study, because it would need massive numbers of patients and cost millions of pounds. He suggested that I should use what is called a surrogate marker approach; that is, to use a measurement of the extent of artery disease such as the ultrasonic measurement of arterial wall thickness or intima media thickness which was being used in the department of vascular surgery under Professor Andrew Nicolaides, and with which I was already familiar. Andrew agreed enthusiastically to this joint venture. I therefore set about raising the money for what, for me, was an enormous undertaking. We would need research nurses to recruit and follow up patients, statistical support, and co-operation from consultants in other hospitals to recruit their patients into the study to obtain numbers large enough to ensure meaningful results. I recruited the most wonderful research nurse called Clare Poulter. She was the ultimate can-do person, always positive. Staff and patients alike loved her. She worked with me for many years, later on the clinical side. It was joy to work with someone like her. I owe her a great deal. I found a statistical person in Judith Diamond. She was working on-site with the eminent statistician, Jane Wadsworth. Judith, by coincidence, was the daughter of a GP friend of my late father, a Dr Lechner. Drs Hugh Mather from Ealing and Patrick Sharpe from Northwick Park agreed that we could recruit their patients into the study. As we were going to use the drug bezafibrate as our intervention, I approached the pharmaceutical firm Boehringer Mannheim, who made the drug, to fund the study. They were enthusiastic in their support. We had many meetings, and the study was ready to go. Studies like this need a name or acronym. I coined the name SENDCAP; St Mary's, Ealing, Northwick Park Diabetes Cardiovascular Disease Prevention Study. Then disaster struck. Boehringer Mannheim pulled out. I never found out the reason. I managed to get a grant from the North West Thames Regional Health Authority. My patient Richard Tompkins, the founder of Green Shield Stamps, also came to the rescue with funds. I also applied to the British Heart Foundation for a grant, which was successful. We recruited 164 Type 2 diabetic subjects. They were followed for a median period of three years with serial measurements of carotid artery intima media thickness. In addition, the patients were monitored for cardiovascular clinical events and had serial electrocardiograms (ECGs). The ECGs were Minnesota coded, an internationally recognised way of documenting events of heart damage due to ischaemia (lack of blood supply).The ultrasound measurements were carried out in Andrew Nicolaides's department. We were fortunate to have two of the world's most experienced Minnesota coders to carry out the measurement on the ECGs. They were Nancy Keen, wife of Harry Keen, one of the world's great diabetes investigators, and Ceridwen Rose, Geoffrey Rose's wife. This study would be considered tiny by today's standards but for me it was huge, and a great achievement to have conceived it and brought it to fruition. The results were published in the prestigious American journal *Diabetes Care* in 1998 (Fig 21). The drug bezafibrate improved the blood fat levels in the patients. Unfortunately, no significant effects were found on carotid artery wall thickness. However, we found that the drug-treated patients had a lower incidence of ischaemic changes on the Minnesota coded ECGs. These positive results saved the study. When the ultrasound results came back as negative, I was devastated. I was not sure whether the results were negative because the measurements were not properly supervised or because there was genuinely no effect. However, I went round to Ceridwen Rose on a Saturday morning. She was then a widow, as Geoffrey had died in 1993 from colon cancer. She gave me the joyous news that the results had been positive. I felt on top of the world. I could claim that this was the first study in which the progress of cardiovascular disease in Type 2 diabetes had been reduced by an intervention. I presented the study at scientific meetings. It was fairly widely quoted in the literature, but I cannot pretend that it was sufficiently significant to shake the diabetic world. The drug bezafibrate has for the most part been replaced by statins in the prevention of cardiovascular disease.

I will digress on this subject for a moment. The statins revolutionised the treatment of cholesterol disorders and were shown to improve the outlook for people with known cardiovascular disease or who were at risk. Indeed, the government's national director for heart and stroke said that all men over fifty and all women over sixty should be offered a statin. On the other hand, there were various press stories that statins increased cancer risk. 'What was the public supposed to think?' I asked in a letter to *The Times* in July 2007 (Fig 22). In this I tried to give a more balanced approach. I did not feel that the blanket prescription of a drug to a large section of the general population was necessary or desirable. I also wrote another letter to *The Times* in May 2016 defending the statins against what I thought were misleading comments from another doctor (Fig 23).

My next and last clinical research fellow was Jonathan Valabhji. He had been our registrar. He wished to research into the relationship between cardiovascular disease and Type 1 diabetes. Cardiovascular disease is a very significant complication of Type 1 diabetes, and the reasons for this are unknown. Blood lipid levels are usually fairly normal in Type 1 diabetes. However, there had been some suggestion that the composition of the individual components of the proteins transporting the lipids might be abnormal and that they might be more prone to damaging oxidation. The enzyme paraoxonase 1 plays an important role as an antioxidant in preventing the oxidation of low-density lipoproteins (the main cholesterol-carrying particle), a process that is directly involved in the development of atherosclerosis. Jonathan, with the help of Avril McColl and Bill Richmond, carried out detailed biochemical analyses to investigate these factors. He did not find that the activity of paraoxonase 1 was related to the ultrasonically measured arterial wall thickness. I had also become interested in the technique of measuring atherosclerosis in the coronary arteries by means of electron beam tomography. Jonathan used this technique to demonstrate a relationship between total antioxidant status in the blood and the extent of coronary artery calcification in Type 1 diabetes. This was an important finding and was published in the prestigious American journal *Diabetes Care*. Jonathan went on to become a consultant on our unit. Later in his career he became the national clinical lead for diabetes and obesity and was awarded an OBE. I was very proud of him and felt that I had played some role in helping his distinguished career.

My last and possibly most significant research project involved the use of the measurement of coronary artery calcification in Type 2 diabetes. I had become interested in this technique of measuring coronary artery calcium through Professor Gilbert Thompson, one of the UK's, and the world's, experts on lipid metabolism and disorders. This technique was quite widely used in the USA but not in the UK. Its measurement promised to be a good predictor of subsequent cardiovascular events. We set up a joint study with BUPA to document the relationship between coronary calcification and coronary risk assessed clinically in asymptomatic patients with hypercholesterolaemia.

I then decided that this technique could be useful in predicting cardiovascular events in Type 2 diabetes and deciding which subjects might need more, and which less, intensive preventative treatment. This would require a prospective multicentre study. I set about assembling a team to do this. I enlisted the help of Dr Marcus Flather, head of the Clinical Trials and Evaluation Unit at the Royal Brompton Hospital, and Dr Michael Rubens, radiologist at the same hospital, who had pioneered the technique in Great Britain. I was also working with Dr Ian Godsland from our own metabolic unit. Ian was an expert at data gathering, statistics and their interpretation. In addition to staff from Marcus's unit, my old friends Michael Feher and Bill Richmond joined the team, as well as Steve Humphries, professor of cardiovascular genetics at University College. I also had two really outstanding research nurses, Alex Dunlop and Anna Widdowson. These two proved to be brilliant recruiters of patients. Drs Anne Dornhorst and Hugh Mather allowed us to recruit patients from the Hammersmith and Ealing Hospitals respectively. I then applied to the British Heart Foundation for a project grant. I was successful. We named the study the PREDICT study (Prospective Evaluation of Diabetic Cardiovascular events with CT). 589 patients were recruited and followed for a median period of four years. This time, the results were striking. Coronary artery calcium score proved to be a powerful predictor of cardiovascular events in Type 2 diabetes and more powerful than conventional risk predictors. We also identified a group of 23% of our patients who had low coronary calcium score and appeared at low risk for cardiovascular events. We then published the final results in the prestigious *European Heart Journal* (Fig 24). The journal wrote an accompanying leading article on the study which was quite an honour. Although this was a true step forward, the technique never became routine in Type 2 diabetes. There were two main reasons for this. It had become apparent that most people with Type 2 diabetes were at increased risk from cardiovascular disease and therefore most were routinely given statins. The technique was expensive at the time and did involve a dose of radiation, though both of these have reduced over time. It is a remarkable coincidence that I ended up carrying out research into arterial calcification, which my father also spent many years researching.

This concludes the description of my research. It ends on a sad note. Bill Richmond died in a tragic accident while pursuing one of his great passions, fishing on the River Spey on 24th August 2010. Bill also had a life beyond science. He was a great raconteur on the subjects of food and wine. He was an accomplished and respected player of the bagpipes and was much in demand to perform for special occasions. He also composed music for the pipes. He had a wide circle of friends from his hobbies of fishing, shooting, whisky tasting and vintage cars. He was a proud Scotsman, though thoroughly against Scottish independence. He had also formed a Scottish clan in France.

I believe that I had contributed significantly to clinical research as an NHS physician. I had raised funds for and trained seven clinical research fellows. I learnt from my experience in Cardiff, where I had no supervision. I sat down with them each week to go through their results, plan the next studies, ensure that they wrote up their work and presented at meetings. I ensured that the fellows had scientific support. I raised money for four scientists to support them as well as doing their own work. I conceived and brought to fruition two prospective cardiovascular studies. I published about 120 scientific papers. I cannot pretend that I became an international figure in research but can claim to have made a significant contribution. Arriving at St Mary's, I felt liberated from the weight of having to produce research and felt able to generate this spontaneously. It became my hobby. I think it was unusual for NHS physicians to engage in significant research then, and it is very uncommon in today's climate. I think this is regrettable because research adds great interest to clinical work. Furthermore, clinicians can identify the problems which need solutions. My colleague Des Johnston was always very supportive of my research. Many other professors would have seen an NHS colleague doing research as a threat. He did not. The success I had in research was also due to the support and help I received from Ian Godsland, and the research nurses Clare Poulter, Alex Dunlop and Anna Widdowson, and all the research fellows and others who joined the team.

CHAPTER 12

Medical Politics and Achievements at St Mary's

Medical training was run on a fairly informal and unstructured basis. After qualification, doctors did their preregistration house jobs. They might then apply for a senior house officer post. Following this they might choose a speciality and apply for a registrar post in this. After about three years they would apply for a senior registrar post in their chosen speciality. From this they would apply to become a consultant. Junior doctors really had to create their own training programmes. House officer posts were appointed locally at each medical school. At that time, we got to know our students well. It was like a large family. If a student impressed us, we would encourage him or her to apply for our house job. This often worked well, and we had a real say in who got our house job. This of course smacked of the old boy network. However, it was a stimulus for students to work hard on the firms and it gave us a chance to appoint someone we could work with.

In 1995, Sir Kenneth Calman produced a report on modernising medical careers which revolutionised postgraduate training. The senior registrar post was abolished. There was a unified training grade (specialist registrar) with a certificate of completion at the end (CSST) which made the doctor eligible to apply for a consultant post. There was a structured training programme. To control numbers entering the grade, only those with a national training number (NTN) could proceed. The idea was to prevent the situation of "time expired" senior registrars who struggled and sometimes failed to get a consultant post. Eventually the house officer posts were allocated centrally so that consultants had no say in who was appointed to their house officer posts. Senior house officer posts were merged into core medical training. The idea behind much of this was that junior doctors would spend far less time in actual work and more in training. Registrars became almost supernumerary from the service point of view and were almost absent from routine outpatient clinics. Initially there were far more jobs to be filled than there were training numbers. Many posts had to filled by so-called locum appointments for training, which were regarded as second-class jobs. Anyone appointed to one of these would be looking to move to one with a national training number, which compromised continuity of service.

The scheme, which continues with some modification to this day, has resulted in far less clinical experience for registrars in their speciality. Thus, when they become consultants, they often face problems with which they are unfamiliar and which they may face for the first time. The senior registrar stage, much maligned, was actually a good training stage before becoming a consultant. It provided a stimulus to improvement and training would usually be completed at a teaching centre to allow more specialist experience before becoming a consultant. In fact, not many failed to become consultants, and if they did, then there was often a reason why they did not succeed. The structured training programme made it almost impossible to get rid of an unsuitable trainee. As a trainer, if you reported adversely on a trainee this was made to reflect on you, and you were likely to have to keep the trainee for a further period of training. In other words, it was rarely the trainee at fault but either the training or the consultants. After completion of specialist training there was a six-month period of grace before becoming a consultant, with no provision for work after that. Many hospitals lost registrars while having to cope with a steadily increasing number of acute medical emergencies. The allocation of national training numbers was done to control numbers. However, no provision was made for those who wanted to train flexibly with the increasing number of female trainees. Trainees were forced to decide at a very early stage on their chosen speciality. This made changing speciality difficult and removed one mechanism by which, under the previous scheme, numbers could be limited by doctors changing speciality. I was involved in the implementation of these changes. I was the Royal College of Physicians' regional advisor in diabetes and endocrinology to the North West Thames Region (1996–2004), and chairman of the North Thames Regional Training Committee for Diabetes and Endocrinology (1996–2000). I was also elected to the Council of the Royal College of Physicians from 1998–2001, and again from 2003–2006. This was by national election.

I could see why these changes were thought important. However, I did not think that they would improve training and thought that they would reduce clinical experience and continuity of care. My colleague Hugh Mather and I carried out a working survey of what colleagues thought about the changes. This was published in the *British Medical Journal* (Fig 25) and showed that most physicians thought that the impact of these changes would be detrimental to patient care. I also wrote a letter to *The Lancet* in 1997 explaining what I thought was wrong with the new system (Fig 26).

The next major change to happen was the implementation of the European Working Time Directive (EWTD). This reduced the maximum time worked by junior hospital doctors to fifty-eight hours per week, including rest periods in hospital. This reduction in actual service commitment by junior doctors really put an end to the old firm structure. Doctors would now work shifts. This was the only way of dealing with the ever-increasing load of acute general medicine. This load was increasing, at least in part, because of the increasing numbers of frail elderly who could not be looked after at home and who required, care not always necessarily from an acute hospital. When patients were admitted they were seen by the duty team and then moved to an appropriate speciality team, or to where beds were available. The days of the old ward round, which happened when I started as a consultant, were over. We never saw the ward sister and counted ourselves lucky if we could find a nurse to accompany us. This, of course, led to poor communication between nurses and doctors. The emphasis of the medical side was on dealing with the acute intakes. The opportunities for registrars to learn about speciality medicine were greatly reduced because there was no time left for them to do outpatient work. I described these problems in a letter to *The Times* on May 9th 2003 (Fig 27). The BMA junior doctors seemed to consider that their main purpose was training rather than service. I considered that training required practical experience with increasing responsibility with supervision, as I pointed out in a letter to *The Times* in October 2010 (Fig 28). Thus, the role of being a consultant physician was far less satisfying than it had been. When we were on take (covering the emergency admissions) we never knew with whom we would be working. We did not have our own teams anymore. Despite all this, I still greatly enjoyed my time at St Mary's. I was elected chairman of the Trust Medical Advisory Committee in 2000 and continued in this role till 2006. We had monthly meetings, to which all consultants were invited and to which the chief executive, Julian Nettel, came. He was an exceptional chief executive who could empathise with doctors. Attendance was patchy unless hot topics such as car parking were being discussed. I was determined to foster a spirit of co-operation between doctors and management and on the whole, I think we succeeded. St Mary's, before the arrival of the internal market, had been a happy institution with a great esprit de corps. The hospital and the medical school worked well together. In more recent times this sense of working together was far less pronounced. This lessening of the corporate sense was partly due to the fact that St Mary's was now part of the Imperial College group of hospitals, which included the Hammersmith, Charing Cross, Queen Charlotte's and the Western Eye hospitals. Consultants were often working between these. The whole of Imperial suffered from poor, dilapidated and very old estate. The worst of these was St Mary's itself, some of the buildings of which had remained unchanged since its foundation. Various schemes for rebuilding had been planned over many years but none had come to fruition. The latest was a grandiose plan for the Royal Brompton Hospital, which specialised in heart and chest conditions, to sell their valuable site in Chelsea and move to a new building on the Praed Street site. This would result in St Mary's being a major force in London and British medicine. This never happened. The doctors at Royal Brompton never really wanted to leave their base in fashionable Chelsea. Furthermore, the establishment of this major hospital would have relegated the Hammersmith to a subsidiary role. This was anathema to the influential powers at Hammersmith and with Imperial, who always saw the Hammersmith as the centre of their universe, an attitude which continues to this day.

I was very fortunate in that I worked on a very happy and well-run diabetes and endocrinology unit. Initially there were just two consultants, Des Johnston and me. We later appointed Stephen Robinson and Jeremy Cox. Later still we were able to appoint Jonathan Valabhji, whom I had brought up as a registrar and then research fellow. In later years Jonathan became the national lead for diabetes and obesity, as mentioned in the previous chapter. As colleagues, somewhat unusually in medicine, we all got on well and worked well together as a team. We had excellent diabetes nurse specialists who helped look after our patients. We had a metabolic ward in which tests were carried out. We lacked our own dedicated outpatient area, which would have greatly improved our service. In 2006 we had an extremely helpful deputy chief executive called Mary Wells. I explained to her the benefits to our unit of having its own dedicated outpatient area. She agreed with this. I found money in the research fund donated through the late Richard Tomkins and his widow, Elizabeth, and the trust paid for the rest. We thus established our own dedicated outpatient area in which we could do daily clinics and see patients who needed to be seen outside these times. It also housed our diabetic foot service as well as diabetic eye screening. This was a great step forward for us.

I reached the pinnacle of my career when, in October 2006, I was given a personal chair in diabetic medicine at Imperial College. I am sure that this came about through the good offices of my wonderful colleague Des Johnston and that I was awarded this on the basis of the research which I had carried out, which I described in the previous chapter. During the interview which I had for this, I was asked why I had not been a pure academic. I replied that I had modelled my career on Sir John Nabarro, who had combined being both a physician and scientist. I felt incredibly honoured to receive this title. I worked my last year of full-time work at St Mary's as Professor Robert Elkeles. In October 2007 I reached the age of sixty-five. Under the regulations at that time I had to retire. I had up to then continued to do general medical on take and all the duties of a consultant physician. When I retired from full-time work my colleagues arranged a magnificent "Festschrift" day, with great tributes to me and my work over the years by colleagues, followed by a dinner at the Royal College of Physicians.

There was a scheme under which you could retire and "come back". I took advantage of this. I was worried about retiring completely and I enjoyed doing outpatient clinics. I therefore came back to outpatient work, two clinics per week. I then continued to work part-time until 2014. I was then aged seventy-two and I thought it right to retire from clinical work. When I retired for the second time, my colleagues did me the extraordinary honour of getting two plaques made with my name engraved and placed in the entrances to our unit. They put on a great naming ceremony attended by the chief executive, Tracy Batten, Arran, Daniel, Jenny, Kate, Thomas and William (Figs 29–31). I think this was probably the proudest moment of my career to be so valued and honoured by my colleagues.

CHAPTER 13

Retirement

At the age of seventy-two, in 2014, I felt it was time to retire completely from clinical work. I felt that there was something rather unseemly in old men hanging round. Medicine was also changing fast and it was quite difficult to keep up to date. Nevertheless, I dreaded retirement. Work had been my life and major interest. I did not feel able to continue my research since this had come to a natural end with the completion and publication of the PREDICT study. I did have a health problem that year. I had regular checks on my PSA following a transurethral resection for benign prostatic enlargement by Professor Roger Kirby some years before. During that year there was a small rise in my PSA. Roger Kirby considered it significant. He advised a full MRI scan and ultrasound biopsy. The MRI did show an area of cancer, which fortunately was confined to the gland. I then was advised to have the biopsy. For those who have not had one, it is fairly unpleasant, done through the rectum. The biopsy went smoothly enough but immediately afterwards I started to pass blood in the urine. The result was clot retention and inability to pass urine. The nurses tried to pass a catheter, but they could not. I had to be admitted to the Princess Grace Hospital to have a cystoscopy and wash-out under general anaesthetic. We had to walk round to the hospital to find that there was a fire alarm. I had to stand in the street, feeling increasingly uncomfortable as my bladder filled up.

Eventually I was admitted. Roger Kirby was away, and another consultant attended. He also could not get a catheter into my bladder and needed a cystoscopy under general anaesthetic. No anaesthetist was available, and I had to wait four hours in agony in urinary retention until one became available. Eventually I had the cystoscopy, and I was able to be discharged the following day. This was one of the most unpleasant experiences of my life. The biopsy came back as positive for prostate cancer. Following this I was asked to have a bone scan. This is part of the routine work-up for prostate cancer. Towards the end of this procedure, the technician looked at it and suggested that I might need a further CT scan. This really scared me.

I got home and was really worried about the possibility of cancerous spread. Quite out of the blue, my old friend Peter Hubner, whom I mentioned before and from whom I had not heard for about a year, phoned for a chat. When I told him that I was in a state of panic he replied that he would offer a prayer for me. Although not religious, I found this profoundly moving and reassuring. As it turned out, the scan was all clear. I underwent a radical prostatectomy at the Princess Grace Hospital. This was where Roger Kirby, one of the country's leading prostate surgeons, worked, using robotic technique. The operation went smoothly. I certainly felt fairly weak for many weeks afterwards. After about two weeks I thought that I would do some exercise on the treadmill in the gym. I felt really ill the next day. I was followed up with regular PSA checks. There was a small rise some months later, resulting in further scans, which were all normal. Since then I have been clear.

Enfield CCG

To keep up my contact with medical matters, I applied in 2012 to join a Clinical Commissioning Group (CCG). I started in 2013. This was one of the bodies set up under the Tories' Health and Social Care Act 2012 under Andrew Lansley, described in Chapter 10. I was appointed as the secondary care doctor on the governing board. The governing board comprised about ten GPs, with a chair, and was supposed to negotiate contracts with local providers to provide services for Enfield residents. This so-called commissioning work was mainly undertaken by administrative staff. My job as secondary care (i.e. representing hospitals) board member was supposedly to provide a secondary care perspective. I found that my role did not really exist. No one was really interested in what I or secondary care thought. The main focus was on the so-called Quality Improvement Programme, which was a euphemism for cost saving. As a CCG we were landed with a historical debt from which we were never able to recover. There were continuing disputes between us, as so-called purchasers, and providers, about how many patients were treated and the prices charged. The amount of time and energy expended in these squabbles seemed quite ridiculous to me. It seemed to me a very inefficient and wasteful way of running the NHS. I also served on the health and safety committee and finance committee. Towards the end of my time I was asked to chair the latter, which I found difficult since I really did not understand the systems and finance has never been my strong card. I had thought that my role would be to act as a link between the CCG and secondary care. I tried to liaise with the medical directors at the North Middlesex Hospital, particularly in relation to their troubled Accident and Emergency department and Barnet and Chase Farm Hospital. I got nowhere. There seemed to be no enthusiasm for my playing any sort of liaison role between the CCG and either hospital. I did not find my role satisfying, nor did I feel I achieved much. Most of the GPs, who were conscientious and hard-working doctors, were demoralised, as they did not feel they were achieving anything on the board and quite rightly felt their time would have been better spent in their own practices. One of the more enjoyable and interesting parts of the initial period was the meeting with secondary care doctors from other CCGs. These were attended by Sir Cyril Chantler. He was one of the pioneers in medical management. He was always full of wisdom and it was a real pleasure to listen to him. These meetings of secondary care doctors seemed to have little influence on the effect of secondary care, at least in my CCG. I served my initial three years and then another three. It was then time to finish. I cannot say that I regretted this. This appointment had served the purposes of giving me some structure to my week and maintaining contact with my profession.

The Peace Hospice, Watford, and St Luke's, Harrow

When I was still working part-time at St Mary's, in 2009, I applied to become a trustee of the Peace Hospice in Watford. I was duly appointed. This seemed to me a very worthwhile cause and one in which I could give something back to society. There were twelve trustees in all, including me. When I was appointed, the chairman was pleasant and effective. He did not interfere in the work of the executive officers. When he retired, he was replaced by one of the trustees. At first everything seemed to continue to run smoothly. I was made chairman of the clinical governance committee. Later on I was asked to be deputy chairman of the hospice. Gradually, over the next few years, it became apparent that the chairman was interfering in the work of the executives. He made life difficult for the director of trading. Running hospice shops is never easy, and on the whole, this director seemed to be doing a good job. The chairman called an extra board meeting for trustees only, in which various allegations were made about the trading director. I could not believe what I was hearing. The director of trading eventually resigned and moved to a similar job at another hospice. I was beginning to realise that there was something very wrong in the conduct of the board. In my meetings with the chief executive, who was generally recognised to be excellent, she made me aware that the chairman was making life difficult for her and it was becoming increasingly difficult for her to do her job. I did my best to intervene on her behalf and asked the chairman to behave differently towards her. Matters came to a head towards the end of 2014. Several members of the board were also becoming increasingly disturbed by the conduct of the chairman. As I was deputy chairman, it was my duty to tackle the issue. This was a difficult time for me, as I had just had a fairly major operation, the radical prostatectomy. I was really not completely well and should not have got involved in this. Anyhow, I did. I wrote a letter, signed by five other trustees, expressing our concerns about his conduct of board affairs and suggesting that we meet. He declined this offer but then sent round an email saying that for personal reasons he would resign from the chair at the next board meeting. Our group was prepared to put forward a substitute chairman. Before the meeting, the trustee who had been most openly critical of the chairman, having sent round a very critical email, resigned from the board. The board meeting was acrimonious. The board was divided. The chairman then withdrew his offer to resign. He was a clever tactician. The opposition to him crumbled and I was left on my own. I did not handle this meeting well and to some extent blame my ill health. I was accused of a gross error of judgement. I replied by saying some board members should examine their own judgements. He therefore remained as chairman. He asked to see me after this, and I was subjected to over an hour of abuse and aggression, the like of which I had never before experienced. The chief executive then resigned and was appointed to another hospice. She explained in detail her reasons for leaving at a board meeting, in which she pulled no punches. When I proposed a vote of thanks to her for all the work which she had done for the hospice I was subjected to a vicious outburst of abuse. I initially thought that I would continue to serve on the board. However, I realised that at least half the board were influenced by the chairman and that I could do little to improve matters. I therefore resigned from the board. I was both amazed and shocked by members of the board who either could not or would not see the obvious mistreatment of perfectly good people. This was an extremely unpleasant affair and something I had not expected at an institution such as a hospice. The Peace Hospice proved anything but peaceful for me.

There is a lesson to be learnt. When things get difficult, few people are prepared to speak out and hold to their principles. I had previously encountered this on the Council of the Royal College of Physicians. However, in the situation which unfolded at the Peace Hospice it was a question of morals. I was quite prepared to take a stand. How I would have reacted in, for instance, Nazi Germany, I do not know. There, if perhaps more had been prepared to take a stand then perhaps the Nazi disaster could have been avoided. However, it is easy to speak from the safety of our wonderful country. I am not brave when it comes to physical violence and of course, at the hospice all I had to lose was my position as trustee. Evil can only be resisted if enough people are prepared to take a stand. The outstanding broadcaster Suzi Klein described in one of her brilliant BBC TV series, *Music Tyrants and Power*, how the famous German composer, Richard Strauss, even though not apparently a Nazi sympathiser, nevertheless complied with the regime to preserve his position as the leading German composer, and also because his daughter-in-law was Jewish.

I was still keen to continue with work for a hospice. I was appointed as trustee to St Luke's Hospice, Harrow. This was a much happier institution. The trading director, HR director and finance director of the Peace Hospice all ended up at St Luke's. I continue at St Luke's to this day. I am again chairman of clinical governance. At the time of writing we are living through the Covid-19 pandemic. This, of course, has hit all charities very hard. Our shops have been shut and charity events cancelled. The shops have, at the time of writing, now reopened. I have just completed a charity bike ride on my own and managed to raise over £1600 for the hospice (Fig 32).

Mount Vernon Hospital Comforts Fund

In June 2019 I was asked to take over the chair at the Mount Vernon Hospital Comforts Fund. This comprised a shop selling newspapers, confectionery and gifts, a bookshop and "look in" shop selling clothes and bric-a-brac, a tea bar in the radiotherapy department and a trolley service to the wards. Money from these outlets went to fund equipment and facilities at the hospital for the benefit of patients attending Mount Vernon Hospital. The outlets were staffed by volunteers who were all dedicated and enthusiastic. There was a board of trustees. The chairman had been in post for about fifteen years and wished to retire. Some of the trustees were members of the U3A walking group, to which Arran and I belonged. I was asked whether I would consider taking this on. I went to see them, was interviewed and asked to become chairman. I continue to do this. At present, because of the coronavirus lockdown, the outlets are shut but we are currently reopening some of our outlets. The charity is run by a really excellent administrator called Lesley Almond, who is highly efficient and with whom it is a pleasure to work.

Cycling

I have enjoyed cycling for many years. I was introduced to it by my good friend Anthony Hewlett. When we were younger, we used to enter a moderate distance charity event each year such as London to Oxford, Cambridge or Southend. We even did the Wessex 100, which was Salisbury to Bath and back. Now, having reached the age of seventy-eight, I cycle several times per week, doing between ten and twenty miles. I find this invigorating and feel very fortunate to be able to do it.

Fig 33 shows Anthony and me at the end of a local charity ride for the Michael Sobell Hospice.

Music

When I was fifty-nine, I ruptured my Achilles tendon playing tennis. At first, I thought I was fine, but it got worse. I went down to A&E at St Mary's, where my colleague Robin Touquet, the A&E consultant, examined me and called down Roger Marston, the orthopaedic surgeon. He immediately said that without an operation I would never play tennis again. I was therefore admitted to the Princess Grace Hospital, where he repaired the tendon. Following this I was in plaster for about eight weeks. During this time, I reflected that in a few years I would have to retire. I had no real hobbies, so I would have nothing to do. I decided therefore to take up a musical instrument. I wanted one which involved playing with others. I mentioned in the chapter on schooldays that my parents encouraged me to play the piano. I did not enjoy it at the time. The piano is generally a lonely instrument. I really loved the sound of the cello, which I decided to take up. I found a teacher in Northwood called Juliet Millen and started. I obviously had some background in music but had forgotten it all. Many people thought this would be too difficult. It has certainly been that. Although I am musical, I found that I was a slow learner at the cello. I have found it difficult, particularly in the co-ordination between brain and hands. Shortly after I started, a patient attended my clinic at St Mary's. He turned out to be Keith Harvey, a renowned English cellist. In conversation I mentioned that I had recently started playing the cello. He said that I should try grade 8. I said that I was just learning. He replied that "We are all just learning and, in any case it is an impossible instrument." Needless to say, I did not follow his advice. Juliet went on maternity leave and I found another teacher locally. He was rather unsympathetic and when he went abroad, he passed me to one of his pupils. I learnt with her for some time. I then decided after this to find a new teacher. By this time, I was playing in an elementary orchestra called the Watford Workshop Orchestra. When I first started, I could hardly play a note. I very slowly improved but still considered myself a poor player. I also joined a group called Pinner Strings. This was an informal group run by a remarkable lady called Hilary Holloway. She had started the group in her front room, and it had gradually increased in size to become about twenty string players. Once again, when I first started, I could only play a few notes. One of the cellists was a lady called Barbara Ferguson. She was also a piano teacher. She recommended me to a new teacher called Margaret Powell, with whom I learn today. She is Australian. She won a Casals scholarship to study cello in Barcelona. She also studied with Jacqueline du Pré. Margaret is a wonderful and inspirational teacher and under her tutelage I have greatly improved over the years. I had a colleague at the Wellington Hospital called Martin Sarner. He was a gastroenterologist and had been one of the London 12 mentioned earlier. He was a highly gifted pianist who could have pursued either music or medicine as a career. He told me when I first started that "I would never do it". I have been trying hard to prove him wrong ever since! He had a big private practice and knew several leading musicians. On one morning we were both doing a clinic in adjacent rooms at the Wellington. He knocked on my door and asked me to come into his room and meet his friend Ralph, who was visiting. Ralph turned out to be Ralph Kirshbaum, one of the world's greatest cellists. Martin introduced me as a "budding young cellist"! I decided to do the grade exams. I gradually, year by year, worked up from grade 3 to 7. I decided not to try for grade 8 as I found the preparation very time consuming and distracting from other playing. I had to learn grade 5 theory and was taught this by Barbara Ferguson. When I did the grade 5 theory exam, I was in a huge examination hall in central London. I think I was the only adult present. Most of the youngsters walked out after about an hour or less. I took the full two hours. I did get a merit. On another occasion, taking one of the grade practical exams, I was waiting to be called in when the person in charge asked, "Where is your child?"

I found the exams very stressful and that my bow arm would tense up and shake. This was really difficult to overcome. Stress levels were high. I currently play in three amateur orchestras: the St Albans evening rehearsal orchestra, Chorleywood Orchestra and Pinner Strings. I have been playing now for nineteen years. It has taken me a long time to achieve even being modestly competent. I am still not good at sight reading new orchestral music. I am better if I have time to prepare. At St Albans, the conductor, Dr Martin Georgiev, who is also a composer, encourages members to play a solo with the orchestra. I have plucked up courage and performed three. The first, far too ambitious, was the adagio from the Haydn cello concerto in D major. The following year I played the slow movement of the cello concerto by JC Bach. This was better. Last year I played the Romance from the cello concerto by Carl Stamitz. This was the best so far and I received very favourable comments about it. I am really grateful to Martin for his support and encouragement in helping to perform these works. I found that playing these solos was more stressful than anything I had encountered in my professional life.

The Chorleywood Orchestra is great fun and we do give public concerts in the Memorial Hall at Chorleywood, which audiences really enjoy. It was started by a highly talented amateur musician and businessman, Andrew McFarlane. The conductor is Richard Wainwright, a professional horn player, who makes rehearsals fun and something to which to look forward.

Pinner Strings is another highlight in my life. When I first started, I could hardly play a note. Now I generally sit in the front row. I often sit next to Anthony Hewlett, mentioned before in the cycling context. He is an accomplished cellist. We meet every two to three weeks in term-time. Hilary Holloway, who built it up, retired in April 2019. She had done everything from conducting, arranging the venue, finding music and the finances, and providing teas. When she retired, I could see that it would fold if no one took it over. I volunteered to be chairman and formed a management committee. After an initial hitch, we now have an outstanding music director, Robert Puzey, and everyone really enjoys the sessions.

Some years ago, I met, at the funeral of Richard Beard, the professor of obstetrics at St Mary's, a previous colleague, Rodney Rivers, who had been an eminent paediatrician. We talked about music. Rodney is an accomplished pianist. Ever since, he has regularly come to our house and we play duets. We also have had a piano trio with violinist Kate Durham, whom I met at the Watford Workshop Orchestra. Towards Christmas each year, Rodney and his wife, Sue, arrange a soirée at their house for all of Rodney's friends with whom he plays. We take it in turns to perform and it is a great occasion. At the time of writing, all these musical activities are in a state of abeyance due to the lockdown following the coronavirus pandemic, but may gradually restart over the next few weeks and months.

Thus, the cello now plays a major part in my life. I can realistically say of myself, as the great Roman writer Tacitus said of a general, that "his ambition was greater than his ability".

I have a weekly lesson with Margaret Powell and start each day with an hour of practice. I am hoping to survive long enough to improve a great deal further. It has given me a new aim and purpose in life.

Walking

Arran and I are members of our local U3A (Northwood) walking group. This meets twice per month, although it has been in abeyance since the lockdown. This is very efficiently run by a lovely couple called Janet and Kerry. One walk is about five to six miles and the other seven to eight miles. Arran is a better and keener walker than I, but we greatly enjoy seeing new scenery in the company of the group. The group usually arrange a walking weekend in the autumn which we have also enjoyed.

History

Since my poor general education at school I have felt extraordinarily ignorant about history. In retirement I have strived to improve my knowledge since I find history fascinating. We joined our local U3A history group which meets once a month.

I have also attended some really stimulating and informative history courses at the adult learning institution called City Lit in Holborn. I have attended courses on modern British history and the Ottoman Empire. Most recently I have been on courses on Imperial Germany and the Weimar Republic. The lecturer on the latter was perhaps the most stimulating lecturer I have ever heard. I was spellbound. This, of course, had great resonance with me as my father Arthur lived through this period.

CHAPTER 14

Family Life

I need to start this with a heartfelt tribute to my life's companion, Arran. She gave up a promising career to support me and the children. After we were married and moved to Cardiff, she worked for eighteen months as a prosecuting solicitor in the Chief Prosecuting Solicitor's office and resigned two weeks before our son, Daniel, was born in 1973. Maternity leave was only a few weeks in those days and part-time work had not been invented. Daniel was one of the first babies to be born at the new Heath Hospital in Cardiff. So, he could have played rugby for Wales. We later discovered that he detested rugby, though amazingly his younger son William excels at it, captains a school team and was voted best rugby player in his school.

Arran was on a career break when we moved back to London in 1975. Our daughter, Jenny, was born in 1976. When Jenny was eighteen months old, Arran started a part-time masters' degree in law and sociology at Brunel University. She had just started her second year when at the end of November, her mother, Mylle, died suddenly of a pontine haemorrhage, aged sixty-one. Mylle had been running the family business on her own following the death of her husband, Henry, just over a year earlier. Mylle's death meant that Arran and her sister Ronnie (Veronica) inherited the company. Arran had never wanted anything to do with the business, but shortly before Christmas the company's employees sent Arran and Ronnie the most enormous bouquets of flowers. Not wanting to let the staff down, they felt they had no option but to continue the business. Arran dropped out of her masters' for a year in order to find the time. Ronnie continued to work as a surveyor for the GLC.

The business was called Acme Flooring Ltd. The office and factory were in Huntingdon near Cambridge. The company manufactured Acme anti-skid panels, which were plywood panels coated with epoxy resin with calcined bauxite chips on top to give a non-skid surface. This was a patented product invented by Henry, Arran's late father. The panels were used on a number of road bridges in London, including Tower and Hammersmith bridges. They were also used on walkways along the Thames and in other places requiring a non-skid surface, such as factories and stations. Arran and Ronnie visited the factory once a week and Arran spent a lot of her time on the telephone to the staff (there was no email in those days). After a year they realised that the business needed more full-time help and expertise than they were able to offer. An advertisement for a managing director produced one good candidate who had just finished an MBA at Cranfield. Arran telephoned him on the evening of the interview to offer him the job. He turned it down, saying he was interested but he wanted to work for a larger company. Then he asked whether she knew someone called Dr Elkeles. Arran told him he was her husband. The candidate told her that he had been seen by Dr Elkeles as a patient, said that he knew exactly the kind of person they needed for their job, and offered to advertise it on the Cranfield notice board for free. The result was the appointment of a managing director who ran the company for the next four years, with Arran and Ronnie taking the role of executive chairmen, and then bought it from Arran and Ronnie as a management buy-out.

Shortly before Acme was sold, Arran had started work as a government lawyer in the Lord Chancellor's department. This was followed by jobs in the department's headquarters working on policy initiatives and Bills, and then a secondment to the Building Research Establishment (BRE) in Watford as head of personnel. She left the civil service and stayed with BRE as personnel director after it was privatised. A couple of years later she left BRE to join a small, niche employment and HR consultancy. After nearly five years' experience with that, she left to start her own employment law, HR and mediation consultancy. She ran that for nearly twelve years until she retired.

Like me, Arran tries to keep herself busy in retirement. Through one of my contacts, she became a trustee of Citizens Advice, Hertsmere, and then became their chair. She also tries to keep her brain active by attending courses at the V&A and City Lit and participating in various activities with our local U3A group. Arran loves to help people. She is a volunteer mediator and conflict coach for Mediation Hertfordshire. She has scored some notable successes in bringing people together and helping them find a way forward and many have been very grateful for her help. In addition, she is a member of our synagogue bereavement support group.

Arran had a portfolio career. It is to my regret that I stood in the way of what would undoubtedly have been an outstanding career in the law. She might well have become a high court judge or more. I have always considered her to be more intelligent than me. However, at the time we married it was usual for the woman's career to play second fiddle to the man's. Today we might have arranged things differently. In the event, she made the best of the circumstances, including having to take over the family business, which had never been her intention. She devoted her life to being the most devoted, caring and loving wife any man could have desired. For this I will be eternally grateful. Whatever I achieved as set out in this account, I could not have done without her. She devoted herself to looking after me and our children and, of course, did the lion's share of care.

Our son Daniel was born in Cardiff in 1973. He was not an easy child. He went to St Martin's prep school in Northwood. He was not an outstanding student. He struggled with Latin. On one occasion I decided to help him with his homework. I had done Latin at A level. He came home the next day and in the margin of his book was written, "Well done Daddy". The headmaster was later found to have abused some of the boys, happily not Daniel, and was dismissed. Following this, I was asked to join the board of governors of the school. I did this for some time but found it too time consuming.

Daniel went on to Merchant Taylors' School, which is at the bottom of our garden. Daniel really came into his own with the Duke of Edinburgh Award scheme, in which he excelled. He became an Award leader and remains good friends with one of the masters involved. Daniel excels at organising and is a real leader of people. He became very good at history. He was awarded a place at Pembroke College, Cambridge, to read history. I well remember the day when Arran and I took him to Cambridge for the first time. It was quite a painful experience for us to see our son leave our care and I admit that I did shed a tear. I am, in fact, a rather emotional person. Daniel thrived at Cambridge. We enjoyed visiting him and taking him out to Sunday lunch at various hotels. He achieved a 2:1 in history. He was offered places on the Sainsbury's and NHS management schemes. He chose the NHS scheme. While he was at school, I arranged a placement for him with the Paddington and North Kensington Health Authority with the help of our wonderful district general manager, Barbara Young (now Baroness Young of Old Scone).

He has made his career in the NHS. He has worked his way up and is currently chief executive of Epsom and St Helier NHS Trust. I cannot say it has been easy for him and he certainly has had setbacks, coming across some really difficult people. He has been on local and national media several times in relation to his attempts to achieve the building of a new hospital to provide new acute services, which are currently provided in the ancient and crumbling buildings of his present hospitals. He has also been on the media in relation to the current Covid-19 pandemic and the opening of a new rehabilitation facility for Covid patients, the Seacole unit, named after the pioneering nurse Mary Seacole. Daniel is resilient, determined and thoroughly dedicated to the NHS and the welfare of patients and staff. I am constantly amazed at how he deals with seemingly insoluble problems, such as when there was a complete lack of Personal Protective Equipment (PPE) at the height of the coronavirus pandemic. He puts great effort into keeping his staff engaged. One story illustrates this. Richard Paisey, who had been my registrar at Northwick Park and had recently retired as consultant diabetologist at Torquay, was carrying out a visit to the Epsom Hospital diabetic foot service. As he sat down at their meeting, he was told spontaneously that their chief executive normally attended but could not on that day. They all remarked on what a popular chief executive he was. I think this bears tribute to Daniel's achievements at his trust. I am hopeful that Daniel will become a leader of the NHS in the future. He is a remarkable man and a very devoted son, husband and father.

In 2000, Daniel married Kate Gray. She is an accountant. She is a highly competent and intelligent lady. She is a wonderful wife for Daniel and a devoted mother. She works almost full-time at a large engineering conglomerate called WS Atkins, which is in Epsom, not far from their home, and is in charge of the IT department. Their first son, Thomas, was born in 2004 and their second son, William, in 2007. The two boys are quite different, but they are a very happy family. Both boys excel at rugby. William has been captain of his team and voted best rugby player in his school. Thomas is on his A level courses and has become enthusiastic about his subjects, history, politics and biology. He is highly articulate and I think could well be a politician. William is an amazing all-rounder who seems to excel at almost everything, including music. He puts enormous effort into all that he does. Both boys are amazing cooks. They live in Reigate. We do not see them very often as the M25 motorway is a significant barrier due to the volume of traffic. They bought a run-down house which we thought would be impossible to renovate. They have confounded all our fears. Kate especially is brilliant at DIY and the house is now magnificent. Kate's parents, Alistair and Beth, have always lived fairly close by and have given considerable help with childcare, and Alistair is also very handy with DIY.

Our daughter, Jenny, was born in Northwick Park Hospital in 1976. She was generally easier to manage as a child than

Daniel. When we moved to Moor Park, she went to St Helen's junior school and then moved on to the senior school. It would be fair to say that she never achieved her full potential at school. St Helen's probably was not the right school for her. She decided that she wanted to read psychology at Bath. She did not achieve the required grades for Bath and got a place at Reading. Here all students took three subjects to start and she chose psychology, philosophy and history of art. She loved the philosophy and took her degree in it. She started off in a hall of residence but moved to what we thought was a really run-down house with other girls, which she really enjoyed. She really enjoyed the course and achieved a 2:1. She never really knew what she wanted to do for a career. After university she did a law conversion course at the London College of Law. She got a job at King's College Hospital in the complaints department. After some time there she moved to the Parliamentary and Health Service Ombudsman. She spent many years there, becoming quite senior and obviously doing well. However, after some years, the whole organisation became very unhappy and poorly led. It seemed likely, at least partially, to close. She moved to the Royal Free Hospital to deal with surgical complaints. After about a year she moved to the Camden and Islington Mental Health Trust, where she handled inquests and claims against the trust. She then got a job at the British Medical Association, where she spent about a year. She then landed a really good job at the East London Foundation Trust. Her role is to handle the large number of inquests and claims against the trust. It is a very large trust, covering large sections of London and extending to Bedford. Almost as soon as she started, the coronavirus lockdown happened. Thus, she has worked at home till the time of writing. The job seems to be incredibly busy and of course she has had no face to face contact with people. Jenny lives in a lovely ground floor flat in West Hampstead which has a beautiful small garden, which she tends with great care. I am very close to her. She is a very loving daughter and the apple of my eye. As she is more accessible than Daniel and on her own, we tend to see more of her.

I shall now relate the sad saga of my sister Marion. In Chapter 6, I explained how she was living in the West Hampstead flat (Acol Court) with her partner Frank. He developed Parkinson's disease. Over the next few years this became steadily worse. His sister and her husband in Bognor Regis did nothing to help. His GP was useless and because he was such an inoffensive man he tended to be ignored when he attended the hospital clinic. I managed to get him seen by one of my colleagues at St Mary's and he started receiving more effective treatment. At the time when our daughter-in-law Kate had just given birth to Thomas, Marion had a bad varicose ulcer on her leg. The district nurses were not really helping. We were just visiting Kate in hospital that evening when Marion phoned me on my mobile, which was very unusual. She was in obvious discomfort. I went round the following day and found her ulcer to be infected. I arranged for her to be admitted to St Mary's, where she was very well looked after by my colleague Jeremy Cox. One evening she phoned me from the hospital saying that she was short of breath. I told her to report this to the staff. She had developed a pulmonary embolus (clot on the lung), which happens when people are immobile. She was taken to ITU, where she miraculously recovered.

We had increasing problems with them both. Frank became increasingly incapacitated. He was sometimes incontinent. We arranged for carers to go to the flat. They found Frank on one occasion naked in the kitchen. Marion also had problems with incontinence and the flat always smelt of urine. The whole situation of them living independently in the flat was becoming increasingly difficult. Sometime in 2012 Marion developed bleeding from the rectum. She, of course, denied this at first. I managed to get her seen by Mr Paul Ziprin, the colorectal surgeon. It was always a huge problem to get Marion to come to the hospital. She underwent tests and was found to have ano-rectal cancer. This would involve major surgery and a colostomy. We had great worries about how she could cope with this. To leave this cancer without treatment would have led to a slow and unpleasant death. With great difficulty we persuaded her to undergo the operation. On the day of the operation, she decided against it and discharged herself. We again persuaded her and she was readmitted. This time, they went swiftly ahead without too much discussion. I remember visiting her the day after this major operation. Others in the ward were lying flat out. She was sitting up reading a magazine. While Marion was in hospital, we phoned the flat one evening to check on Frank. He was not there. I immediately went to the flat. I phoned A&E at the Royal Free and found Frank there. We got him home with the help of Jenny, who collected him.

It became clear to us, especially to Arran, that they could no longer live safely in the flat and that residential accommodation was needed for both of them. We eventually found a care home, near our home, in Oxhey, called Pinewood Lodge. They accepted Marion as a paying resident. Frank's situation was different. He had no means. Somehow, we managed to persuade the council to pay for his care in the same home. It took a great deal of persuasion and guile to get Marion to accept that she could not return to Acol Court. In the end, we succeeded. Once we got her there, she kept asking when she was going home and what was going to happen next. Frank was housed in the dementia part, since he had developed a degree of dementia. We thought that they would be happy together in the same home. However, Marion lost interest in Frank and seemed keen on another resident, who did not reciprocate. Frank deteriorated fairly quickly thereafter and died. Happily, his relatives did at least arrange for his funeral. Marion did not seem particularly upset at his death. She did not seem to have deep emotions. She was not happy at Pinewood. I think she was very difficult to deal with. She was resistant to being washed and the staff had the greatest difficulty in keeping her clean. We had experienced this problem before at Acol Court. She would not take part in any of the activities put on by the staff. She did not like the food. It was sad for us to see that she was unhappy there. However, it seemed that it was the best we could arrange. I tried to give her some pleasure by taking her out on trips to the Aquadrome at Rickmansworth, where she enjoyed a coffee and a cake. In 2013, staff noticed a recurrence of her cancer. She was seen again at St Mary's, where it was confirmed that the cancer had recurred. This presented a big dilemma. It was, of course, impossible to discuss any options with her. Any possible treatment would be extremely distressing and difficult. Leaving the cancer untreated would likely result in an unpleasant and painful death. Nature came to our rescue. She went downhill fairly quickly. She was admitted to Watford General Hospital. It seemed that she had developed some sort of pneumonia. After some hours I was told that she was unlikely to survive. She apparently staged a comeback, only to relapse. She died in Watford Hospital the following day, 24th May 2014. Thus ended a sad life. Nevertheless, it was a relief for us and, I think, for her. She had had some happier days with Frank at Acol Court, but her quality of life latterly was very poor. She was cremated at Golders Green Crematorium on Sunday 1st June, my birthday. There was a small gathering. My dear friend Richard Thompson came to support me, for which I was very grateful. I gave a short address describing her life and ending, 'Marion is now at peace and does not have to suffer any more. For this I am profoundly grateful.' We had a family picnic in Kenwood Park.

The whole saga of Marion had been very difficult. My father Arthur saved hard for her to be looked after and he succeeded. She never lacked the means. In looking after her I received huge support from Arran, and also Jenny, and moral support from Daniel.

I turn now to our life as a family. I think that we were a happy family. Our home in Moor Park was a happy one. Interestingly, the house which we bought in Moor Park had once belonged to the famous ventriloquist Peter Brough, whose puppet was called Archie Andrews. When Daniel and Jenny were small, we went on family holidays. We went on several French language holidays. These were called Accents First, in Artemare, between Lyon and Geneva, and later in Forcalquier, in Haute Provence in South West France, run by a couple called Pam and Alain Bourgeois. We drove down to these places. Once there, the guests were made to feel part of the local village. I think we enjoyed them but especially Arran, who is almost fluent in French. On our first trip we met a family with whom we have remained friends. They were Tom and Beth Batey. They had two sons, Dan and Jamie. They were from Aberdeen. Tom is an eminent soil scientist and Beth was a social worker. Tom spent twelve years in the state advisory service based at Cambridge and Reading. He then spent seventeen years in academia in the University of Aberdeen, teaching soil management and land use at undergraduate and postgraduate level. He has worked independently, advising major farming groups in countries around the world. They are a truly wonderful couple. Some years ago now, their younger son, Jamie, died from a progressive brain tumour. He had suffered for some years. We remain in regular contact with Tom and Beth.

We had some other holidays, some in England and one in Menorca, which was extremely hot. This was memorable for a restaurant we enjoyed called Chez Gaston, which served a delicious gazpacho. We did try a few skiing holidays, one with Peter and Sandra Hubner and family. Our children never really took to skiing and of course, Arran hated the whole thing. One winter I was allowed to take Daniel on my own on a skiing holiday. We went to the fashionable ski resort Lech, in Austria. When we got there, I realised it was a mistake. Daniel missed his mum. I took him up on the chair lift. We had just got going when I realised he was not properly strapped in. To my horror he dropped off to the ground. I was petrified and thought the worst had happened. I had to reach the top and ski down. Miraculously, he was uninjured. This certainly gave me a bad fright. I did persuade him to join some classes, which I think he enjoyed. Skiing never became a favourite of the Elkeles family. I was the only one who enjoyed it.

We then tried some time share holidays in Britain. After several, we found what we thought was our ideal. This was Craigendarroch in Ballater in Royal Deeside, near Balmoral in the Scottish Highlands. We bought a large chalet for the first two weeks in August. The chalets were luxuriously appointed; there was a leisure complex and restaurants. The scenery in Aberdeenshire is stunningly beautiful and for us, was probably better than the Swiss Alps. We spent our time walking and sight-seeing. Jenny was not keen on this and called me the "chairman of the boring walks association." There were also interesting castles to see and, of course, spectacular scenery. The year we bought it the weather was beautiful and hot. We went back the following year and it rained continuously. It was miserable. We returned one more time, but the children really did not like it. We had some different holidays. After Daniel's marriage to Kate and when they had the two boys, they expressed interest in coming up. We bought them their own time share. They used this once or twice. However, there was not enough to keep the boys amused, the weather could be miserable and the journey was long. Eventually they sold it. We also decided to sell. This was not easy. We put it on the market. After a year the agent called to say that someone was interested in buying one of our weeks. We went up, supposedly for the last time. The weather was sunny and warm. I cycled up and down the River Dee and we again appreciated the beauty of the scenery. We thought it was crazy to sell it and we took it off the market. Thereafter we had many years of really enjoyable holidays there. It was a long drive, about 500 miles. On the way up we used to stay in Lancaster at the Lancaster House Hotel. On the return we usually drove home without stopping. The walking was excellent and varied and we were able to use several good local walking guides. On one occasion we were walking in the hills above Balmoral and met Prince Charles and his security man, who gave us a friendly greeting. On another occasion we were walking in the same hills on a track when a Land Rover suddenly appeared behind us. We looked round and found that the driver was the Queen. We were not invited in for tea! We climbed Lochnagar (the highest local peak) several times. We made friends locally. We renewed our friendship with Tom and Beth Batey. It was always a joy to be with them. Tom was a very good and experienced walker and an expert navigator, and we had many spectacular walks with them. They sometimes stayed in our time share. We were fascinated by the fishing villages on the North East coast such as Buckie, Cullen Findochty, Portsoy and Banff. They had a sort of 'passé' and eerie atmosphere about them which we found attractive. To reach them, it was a long but spectacular drive over the Highland passes, passing through the ski area known as the Lecht. We felt our holiday would not be complete without a visit to the North East coast. In the Cairngorms near Aviemore there is Loch Morlich, which actually has a sandy beach, very tempting on a sunny day, of which there were not too many! I also had a sailing lesson on Loch Insch in the Cairngorms, which was rather a long way to drive for this. I was a bit crazy! The locals in Ballater organised a Ballater walking week in May. We went on this and were so impressed that we bought an extra week's time share to coincide with it, having been told the week would remain unchanged. However, after a year they changed the week so that our time share week no longer coincided with it. We therefore did sell this extra week. The walking week had three levels of walking: easy, medium and hard. On the second holiday I judged myself to be fit and tried the hard group. On the first day we climbed three Munros (mountains over 3000 feet) and on the second, Lochnagar, over a boulder field. I do not know how I survived this workout. I realised I was not up to this and opted again for the medium group!

Ballater itself is not a particularly picturesque village. Down the road from Craigendarroch was the McEwan art gallery. We regularly visited this and bought several paintings by Scottish artists, which hang in our lounge at home. During the first few years of our stays, there was a really good restaurant called the Green Inn at which we sometimes ate. When this closed there wasn't anywhere we liked. Of the two restaurants at Craigendarroch itself, one was geared for children and the other expensive and pretentious. During the first week in August the locals put on 'Victoria Week' with several interesting events including a special walk, a concert, an evening talk etc. On one such walk, Arran met a lady called Ruth Hieghton Jackson. She was married to a retired naval officer, Doug. We became friends and spent many enjoyable evenings together and remain in contact. Doug and Ruth left Ballater some years ago and now live in Dorset. We were at their house in Ballater one evening when they received a phone call that one of their two sons, who was an army officer serving in Afghanistan, had been injured by a bomb. Happily, he was not seriously injured. He did, however, suffer damage to his middle ear, which has badly affected his balance and hearing ever since. We made several friends there over the years. We also met up with Lord Simon Glenarthur and his wife Susan. Simon had been chairman of the St Mary's Hospital Trust board and I had got to know him then. He was a very supportive chairman and often went round the wards himself. I remember one occasion, when I was busy reading some notes on the ward, when there was a tap on my shoulder, and it was Simon enquiring how things were going. Simon and Sue had a beautiful farmhouse in Banchory. We were invited to dinner there and they also came to us each year. Aberdeen is an interesting city with a spectacular coast. Tom and Beth often took us to the Sands of Forvie, vast stretches of golden sands. On a hot day you could easily imagine being in the South of France.

We bought the time share in 1989. By 2013 we felt we had had it long enough and finally decided to sell. We had had it for twenty-four years. We had many really good holidays out of it. Our abiding memories will be of the stunning scenery of Aberdeenshire and Moray, which for us surpasses anything we saw in Europe. The sale of our time share at Craigendarroch ended an important episode in our lives. Apart from these time share holidays in August, when Daniel and Jenny had left home we often went on a walking holiday in May. Initially these holidays were with a company called Alternative Travel Group (ATG). These were quite upmarket and well organised trips in which a group of about sixteen people walked from one place to another. We started with trips in Northern Italy, in Tuscany and Umbria. We visited places such as Volterra and San Geminiano. The walks could be strenuous, and it was often very hot. The ATG staff were usually outstanding and prepared a picnic en route at lunch time. We were usually put up in reasonable hotels overnight before walking on the next day. In all we did over ten of these trips. After that we joined Holiday Fellowship, or HF, which arranged group walking holidays, mainly in England. The groups were always fun, and it was rather cheaper than ATG. We went to Alnmouth in Northumberland, Dovedale in the Peak District, Abingworth on the South Downs and St Ives and Freshwater Bay on the Isle of Wight. We also bought a share in the Holiday Property Bond company. This gave us holidays in various well-appointed country houses over Britain and Europe. We did several such holidays, including two in France. However, they were self-catering, which, quite reasonably, Arran found tedious, and lacked the company of other people, which we always enjoyed. Furthermore, one had to book at least a year in advance for a suitable time slot in the nicer places. After some years we sold our share in this.

In recent years we were introduced to ACE Cultural Tours. These are upmarket group tours with a cultural theme, with a mainly elderly clientele. They always have an expert tour leader who gives talks and guides the group. We have done the Bath Mozart and Bach festivals, Hadrian's Wall, the Industrial Revolution based in Stoke on Trent, the Golden Age of Dutch Painting in Amsterdam, river cruises on the Seine and Rhône, Shakespeare in Stratford-upon-Avon, Gilbert and Sullivan in Harrogate. A highlight was the music and art trip to New York, in February 2017. February in New York is usually very cold. We had boiling hot sunny weather. When we did the usual trip by boat to the Statue of Liberty and Ellis Island it was like a Mediterranean cruise!

Apart from holidays, we became members of our local U3A, mainly the walking group. We have a circle of friends. Arran is a very good cook, and we give dinner parties which are always popular.

Since we moved to Moor Park in 1981, our next-door neighbours have been Frances and Teddy Button. They have become close friends over the years. We help each other as needed. We could not have asked for better neighbours.

Sir—Philip Barber[1] has written the most honest and balanced review of the true implications of the UK specialist-registrar training programme that I have yet read. "Calman training" will indeed result in certified, clock-watching, didactically trained specialists who will lack initially significant in-depth experience and in no way be qualified to accept the responsibilities or carry out the duties expected by our patients of a traditional hospital consultant. This is appreciated by many of the current specialist registrars themselves, especially those in the surgical specialties. They are terrified at the thought of being appointed a consultant.

The profession can no longer afford to ignore these warnings but the British Medical Association, supported by the Royal Colleges, continues to argue that these trainees must be appointed, at the end of their 4, 5, or 6 years, to a traditional, free-standing consultant post carrying full clinical responsibilities. There was open opposition to a recently advertised "junior consultant" post at Guy's Hospital, London.

The Calman specialist registrars and their Royal College-dictated training programmes are with us, and reversion to traditional prolonged apprenticeship style learning is unlikely and undesirable. However, we must protect patients from the results of a false belief that these clinicians are fully experienced. Barber did not propose a way forward but one approach, which will also overcome the escalating demands on the time of individual consultants and solve some of the hospital-staffing problems, is to review the concept of "the consultant". The stand-alone, omniscient, omnipotent consultant must be replaced with teams of consultants working together, teams that contain colleagues with various levels of experience and varying interests. The junior members, clasping their recently acquired certificates of specialist training, would have the opportunity to take full responsibility for clinical action within their experience. They would gain further expertise by undertaking clearly defined duties, including resident on-call ones, under the umbrella of more senior colleagues who will be readily contactable for advice and help in complex situations.

These junior consultants would thus gain in-depth experience of their chosen specialist clinical practice and have the opportunity for formal training in other non-clinical activities which interest them—ie, undergraduate and postgraduate teaching, research, or administration. They should thus acquire something of the professionalism of consultants trained traditionally during long hours of exciting, challenging, unstructured, and often tiring clinical work in the "bad old days".

By encouraging such changes the Royal Colleges and the BMA would ensure the evolution of a new concept of consultant care which would embrace the highest standards of clinical practice and current political thought, coupled with an acceptable life style for all.

K E F Hobbs

University Department of Surgery, Royal Free Hospital, London NW3 2QG, UK

1 Barber P. The Colleges, Calman, and the new deal. *Lancet* 1997; **350:** 974.

Sir—Philip Barber[1] reflects the view of most consultant physicians on the new training structure for specialist registrars. This has been implemented without consideration of the likely difficulties and without consultation, and it is causing serious problems.

In many specialties there are far more jobs than there are national training numbers (NTN) and many posts have to be filled by locum appointments for training. Trainees regard such appointments as second-class because they need to compete again for an NTN even if they have already been through the interview process. Anyone in such a locum post will try to leave at the first opportunity to obtain an NTN, and this compromises continuity of service.

The former transition from registrar to senior registrar had important advantages. It provided a stimulus to improvement and training would usually be completed at a teaching centre to allow more specialist experience before applying for a consultant post. Under the new system, with doctors entering and leaving schemes at varying and often unpredictable times for research or for other reasons, it it impossible to guarantee jobs at the appropriate centre at the appropriate time.

The new system envisages a 6-month period of grace after completion of training before the certificate specialist registrar obtains a consultant appointment. What happens if they do not obtain a post within this period? With the introduction of this scheme, many hospitals have lost registrars while having to cope with a rising tide of acute medical emergencies. To suggest that this extra work should be met by consultants is unrealistic.[2]

The effects on academic medicine are especially serious. Specialist registrars taking time off for research have to be replaced by locums, which disrupts service, and the difficulties of incorporating university lecturers, who also require accreditation, into the scheme are only now beginning to be addressed.

The heavy work-load administering these training schemes has been largely devolved to the individual training committee (ie, the consultants). The tasks are too great for them to be done in consultants' spare time.

Allocating NTNs to trainees was presumably done to control numbers. Prediction of future needs has always been difficult. There needs to be slack in the system, to take account of trainees who opt for flexible training and of others who may drop out of the system for a time. Trainees are forced to decide at very early stage which specialty they wish to pursue and to change specialty is difficult. This limits experience and removes one mechanism by which, under the old scheme, numbers could be limited by doctors changing specialty.

Robert Elkeles

Unit for Metabolic Medicine, St Mary's Hospital, London W2 1NY, UK

1 Barber P. The Colleges, Calman, and the new deal. *Lancet* 1997; **350:** 974.

2 Mather HM, Elkeles RS. Attitudes of consultant physicians to the Calman proposals: a questionnaire survey. *BMJ* 1995; **311:** 1060–62.

Sir—The commentary by Philip Barber[1] reflects, I suspect, the views of the vast majority of clinicians in the UK. Why have we stood back and watched the high standard and enjoyment of clinical medicine disappearing under non-evidence-based edicts? I suppose because the silent majority of clinicans have been left beleaguered by more voluble ex-colleagues who now dictate to them from the bureaucracies that attracted them out of mainstream care delivery into the seductive political world. What a pity more of us have not taken as much time publicly as we have privately, to express our dismay at the implementation of systems we all loathe and for which we have never accepted the rationale.

There is a further, so far unmentioned, consequence of these harebrained new schemes that may be even more destructive than the schemes themselves. That is the appearance of a reduced threshold for doctors in training to take sick leave. This is likely to be due to reduced morale and commitment rather than increased disease.

Fig 26

LETTERS TO THE EDITOR

1 Pennington Street, London E98 1TA. Telephone: 020-7782 5000
Fax: 020-7782 5046 e-mail: letters@thetimes.co.uk

Tests, tables and school performance

From the Chairman of the Specialist Schools Trust

Sir, Her Majesty's Chief Inspector of Schools, David Bell, quite rightly emphasises the principle of accountability for our schools (report, May 5).

The success of the 1,200 specialist schools which regularly outperform other comprehensive schools with comparable intakes of ability has been built on making them accountable for the extra funding which they receive by requiring them to meet their own targets for improvement.

If accountability is a crucial ingredient of raising performance, so is transparency. Parents should be able to obtain easily understandable, timely data on how their children and their school are performing.

However, clearly it is unfair to compare, using raw data only, the performance of schools in the leafy suburbs with intakes of high-ability children with those in areas of severe social disadvantage in the inner city, many of whose children do not speak English at home.

That is why the Specialist Schools Trust has asked Professor David Jesson to develop an easily understandable value-added measure. Professor Jesson has in each of the past two years been able to match the Key Stage 2 test results of over 90 per cent of pupils in specialist schools with their GCSE results five years later. He is now able to predict what percentage of top grades at GCSE an incoming set of 11-year-olds should achieve, and compare this with the actual result.

Our headteachers accept this as a fair and understandable tool to compare their performance with other schools and to improve learning by setting realistic targets for their children.

Yours faithfully,
CYRIL TAYLOR,
Chairman,
Specialist Schools Trust,
37 Queen's Gate, SW7 5HR.
May 6.

From Mr Ian Foster

Sir, You comment (leading article, May 5) on the distinction between testing and the compilation of performance tables. You also state that there is a case, though not one you necessarily agree with, for the abolition of such tables.

I led the abolition of tables motion at last weekend's National Association of Head Teachers (NAHT) conference. I began by stating unequivocally that we have no problem with testing, within reason. Testing, correctly carried out, informs future learning and teaching. It is the very publication of performance tables, with their frustrating flaws, that continues to germinate the excessive testing regime now predominating. This in turn has led to an education system which has become increasingly prescriptive, to the detriment of creativity.

In the latest available international study on literacy, Finland had the highest score (the UK came seventh). At a recent conference the Finnish delegation put their success down to good teachers who have the freedom to innovate and are trusted. There are no performance tables in Finland.

Yours faithfully,
IAN FOSTER
(Council member, NAHT,
West Midlands),
Leominster Junior School,
George Street, Leominster HR6 8JZ.
May 6.

From Mr W. H. Cousins

Sir, School tests? Yes, if only because, in general, what isn't tested isn't taught.

Unfortunately, with too much testing, education becomes no more than instruction.

Yours sincerely,
W. H. COUSINS,
222 Corbets Tey Road,
Upminster, Essex RM14 2BL.
May 6.

Key to raising local election turnout

From the Chief Executive of the Local Government Information Unit

Sir, The local election turnout (reports, May 3) confirms the Electoral Commission's research finding that 36 discretionary local pilots in proportional representation would help. However, the core issue is the motivation to vote based on voters' perception of the relevance of the democratic process.

Effect of EU rules on doctors' hours

From Dr Robert Elkeles

Sir, The European Working Time Directive (EWTD) will compulsorily reduce the maximum time worked by junior hospital doctors (report, April 22) to 58 hours per week including rest periods in hospital. It has to be fully implemented by August 2004; further reductions are then planned by 2009.

A recent report from the Royal College of Physicians of London documents how this will abolish all residential on-call medical rotas and consign resident trainees of all grades involved in acute medicine to full-shift rotas. Since with present staffing levels this will greatly reduce the hours spent by trainees in the hospital, the change will require at least a 50 per cent increase in the number of middle-grade doctors to maintain a 24-hour service.

Partial solutions proposed include using nurse practitioners and healthcare assistants to undertake some tasks performed by junior doctors, concentrating acute services in fewer units, recruiting more foreign doctors and putting yet more work on consultants. All of these, however, even if practicable, could not make up the shortfall in the 15 months remaining.

Although the supposed rationale for the EWTD is to improve the lot of junior doctors, a recent survey of specialist registrars showed 78 per cent preferring the traditional on-call rota to working in shifts, which are more disruptive to family life, and markedly increase work intensity, while reducing the continuity of care that is increasingly important for patients.

I and my colleagues believe that the shortfall cannot be made up by consultant physicians, who already work an average of more than 60 hours per week, and the Royal College has therefore suggested that the implementation should be postponed at least until these manpower issues can be resolved. Unfortunately the Government has not accepted this assessment and seems determined to implement the changes against medical advice (*Hansard*, March 18, cols 751-53). Can nothing be done to stop it?

Yours faithfully,
ROBERT ELKELES
(Consultant physician),
St Mary's Hospital,
Praed Street, W2 1NY.
May 7.

Fig 27

National Trust and 'Disneyfication'

Sir, I echo Stephen Bayley's dismay at the way the National Trust continues to cheapen the atmosphere around its great buildings (Opinion, Oct 18). But I would add something more. The National Trust has one of the most extensive chains of bookshops in the UK, often in out-of-the-way places where no other bookshops exist for miles around. Instead of developing these in keeping with the trust's high cultural calling, its bookshops are an embarrassment to an intelligent person and contain almost no books of importance. Instead they have been turned into gift shops of cloned stock.

To go to a great house and discover only a small pamphlet on the subject, no serious back-up works on history, architecture and design, and the rest of the space given over to mugs, birthday cards, souvenir chocolate bars etc, is very dispiriting.

DUNCAN FALLOWELL
London W11

Sir, Stephen Bayley seems to think that National Trust buildings should be preserved as carcasses for inspection by architectural historians. He misses the point entirely. National Trust properties were once homes. By furnishing them with artefacts truly revelatory of previous owners' lifestyles, visitors are given historical perspectives of slices of social history which would be almost completely missing from an empty shell. We value historical dramas such as *Downton Abbey* partly for their authenticity and faithfulness to period detail. And therein lies the nub. It is the details, such as the clothes and the kitchen utensils, the upstairs-downstairs experience, which for most of us explain the function of the buildings in which they are housed.

DAVID ESSEX
London SW20

Doctors' training needs v continuity of ca

Sir, There is a balance to be weighed which Dr Tom Dolphin (letter, Oct 16) does not seem to have considered. We are now producing inexperienced and inadequately trained doctors. These doctors will therefore make mistakes — some distressing, some life-threatening and some fatal. Add that the present shift system makes continuity of care a thing of the past, and you have the potential for further mistakes, which too could be fatal.

A great deal is made of trainee doctors working excessive hours. When my late husband trained he was on duty for well in excess of 100 hours every week. For instance, every other weekend on call lasted from Friday morning until Monday evening — about 84 hours — but he was not actually working during all those hours, so had time to rest. These hours, which involved sleeping in at the hospital, lasted only a few years. Yes, he did get tired, but he was young and tough and very soon learnt to catnap. He saw a huge amount of clinical material and received a thorough training, which made him into a fine clinician. As a newly married senior house officer he was told by his senior consultant that on his nights off he was required to come back and sleep in the hospital so that he was available to see any exceptional cases that might crop up in the labour ward.

ANN TURNBULL
Silverdale, Lancs

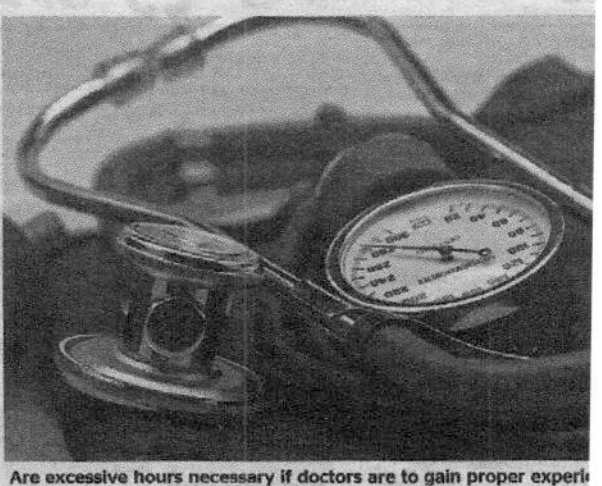

Are excessive hours necessary if doctors are to gain proper experi

Sir, Dr Tom Dolphin and the BMA junior doctors committee do not correctly represent their colleagues. No one is advocating a return to the excessive hours of many years ago. However, we need a balance of sufficient hours to provide for continuity of care for patients to ensure their safety and to provide sufficient experience for junior doctors, neither of which is possible under the present rigid system.

Dr Dolphin wishes us to believe that the sole purpose for junior doctors is training. This cannot be right. Good training needs both theoretical instruction and practical experience with increasing responsibility (with supervision).

Dr Dolphin also points to the dangers of tired doctors. Far more dangerous is the prospect of newly appointed inexperienced consultants having to take difficult decisions on their own for the first time.

ROBERT ELKELES
Consultant physician and Professor of Diabetic Medicine
Northwood, Middx

Sir, Further to Dr John Harty's letter (Oct 18), it might be added that even if the "opt out" from the European Working Time Directive is maintained, Dr Tom Dolphin and his contemporaries, if appoin consultants, may choose t to work a 48-hour averag removing the last vestige continuity of care.

The concept of consult responsibility for the indi patient may need to be re each inpatient then come successive care of even m consultants in that specia combining the roles of co and junior doctor as num juniors diminish (as they further increase in the nu consultants is to be afford necessarily having any m than at present to repeat each other to become ac with each patient's histo being likely to have suffi acquire the level of detai years helpful to understa and advancing managen

DR RICHARD PONSFORD
Thurlaston, Warks

Fig 28

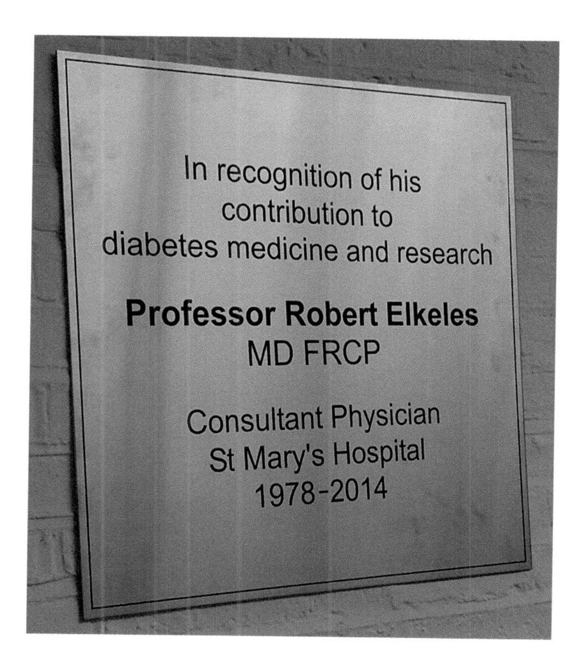

Fig 29

In recognition of his
contribution to

Fig 30

clinell
contribution to
diabetes medicine and research
Professor Robert Elkeles
MD FRCP
Consultant Physician
St Mary's Hospital
1978-2014

Fig 31

Fig 32

Fig 33

1 London Bridge Street
London SE1 9GF
Email: letters@thetimes.co.uk

How to be top

Sir, I am wary of conclusions drawn from statistics outlined in your article about the backgrounds of people in top jobs ("Old boys and girls still take the top jobs", Aug 28).

The statistics do not say how such people came to be privately educated. Some fit the upper-class stereotype, of course, but many do not. Sport is an example. Public schools often offer scholarships to talented individuals who then go on to greater things.

I suspect that a great many people come from ordinary families which, in the previous generation or two, have been successful after a state school education. In turn, they decided to seek what they perceive to be best for their offspring by providing for them a private education.

If we look at the wider backgrounds of these "top" people, a different picture emerges: more people from ordinary backgrounds end up in influential positions than is generally realised, and this is to be applauded.

IAN HALE
Farnham Common, Bucks

Scottish independence, seen from England

Sir, Over the past year I have found myself moving towards being a Yes supporter. I am English, so this is academic, but the more I examine where England is as a nation, the more I am appalled at the failure of socio-economic neo-liberalism that creates a tiny powerful elite while marginalising everybody else.

From housing to welfare to justice, to education to economic fairness we in England are morally skewered. That Scotland has a chance to shake off the legacy of elitism and exclusion is fantastic. In doing so I hope Scotland provides the radical mind shift that we in England so desperately need to embrace fairer ways of doing things.

The earthquake that would come from Scottish independence would force us to rightly look at ourselves and what we truly stand for.

GERARD BROWN
London W2

Sir, Alistair Darling and Gordon Brown heading the No campaign? Where are the English politicians telling Scotland why we want them, why we need them and why they should stay with us?

LESLIE HOWARD
St Albans

Sir, Listening to the Yes campaign one might think that Scots are an oppressed people living in poor conditions. But our island is a haven of freedom and relative prosperity which people risk their lives to join. What sort of paradise do the Scots think they can create by this messy, expensive and divisive divorce?

PROFESSOR ROBERT ELKELES
Northwood, Middx

Sir, It defies logic that Scotland might retain the pound. It would remain hugely dependent on the remaining UK government's economic policy but without any representation. It is better off now.

MICHAEL OLD
Poole, Dorset

Sir, With this recent defection of a Conservative MP to Ukip, the upcoming Scottish referendum and a possible future referendum on EU membership, it is not conceivable that in the near future we could be out of the European Union while Scotland is in.

DAN GREEN
Ewell, Surrey

Sir, I have, like most in England, only had a passing interest in the Scottish referendum but I would be keen to know what the chances are of keeping "English" Summer Time throughout the year if the Scots decide to depart, as I am certain it would improve the road safety of the inhabitants south of the border.

It would be left to the Highland dairy industry to plead directly with Alex Salmond for their historical light-saving advantage that we have afforded them in the past.

STEPHEN WILLIAMS
Saffron Walden

Sir, There are a dozen countries in the EU with populations similar to or smaller than Scotland's. None shows any desire to change its status even if its economy is dependent upon its larger neighbours. The arguments so far have concentrated on the economic disadvantages of a Yes vote. Little regard has been given to national pride or the emotional appeal of self-rule. It would be strange if Scotland were to enter the history books as the nation that rejected independence. Is it not said that it is better to be governed badly by one's own than to be ruled well by strangers?

CHARLES MCCARTHY
Stamford, Lincs

After a long life, a good death?

Sir, While baking my mother's 103rd birthday cake last week I read your report "Four in five doctors would not help patients to end their lives" (Aug 23).

There is an associated aspect of this important ethical dilemma which I believe we, as a society, are ignoring. I applaud Professor Raymond Tallis's advocacy of the "secondary aim" of doctors — the reduction of suffering.

My mother's death has been postponed three times in the past five years by medical intervention which was unavailable to an earlier generation. She suffers increasing levels of pain, discomfort, distress and miserable confusion. This suffering comes after an active, fulfilled and positive life. It is unbearable to watch, and her situation is far from unique.

In a caring society, surely we need sometimes to allow very old people to die, simply offering them pain relief and a peaceful departure from this life?

ROSIE WOOD
Guildford

Recline and tall

slamming their backrest into your knees just make life worse for both of us. Nor is this a special plea for men. I

Tyre by the Hebrew tribe of Asher after its destruction. Significantly, the wreck date coincides with the

Read tide tables

Sir, I am really not sure what the fuss is about mobile signals in this part of Cornwall. I live within 100m of the house where the prime minister has been on holiday and I regularly get a mobile signal on two different

Fig 34

Decline in support for Labour under Corbyn

Sir, David Aaronovitch is right to draw attention to the dire state of the Labour Party ("Corbynism is rotting from the head down", Jul 4). Since it first aspired to power Labour has needed to maintain a balance between an ideological, Marxist-influenced left and a pragmatic social-democratic right. The mood of the time, and the voting changes introduced by Ed Miliband, meant that a candidate of the left would succeed in 2015. Had it been Diane Abbott or John McDonnell I would not have been pleased, but I believe they would have had the motivation and the ability to keep the coalition in place. Sadly the left chose someone who lacks both these characteristics and has no discernable qualities beyond market-place oratory. The consequences are all too apparent.
Martyn Sloman
Labour parliamentary agent for North Norfolk 2015; former parliamentary candidate; Sharrington, Norfolk

Sir, The substantial 2017 Labour vote was in no way indicative of a desire for a Corbyn government. It was to an extent made up of Corbyn supporters, but also largely by anti-Brexiteers who foolishly thought that Corbyn would fight to stop it, and that Labour was the only party that could. The third group of Labour voters were supporters of the non-extremist MPs who wanted Labour to retain a core of recognisable Labour identity. The fourth group were those who would always vote Labour. Corbyn has surfed for three years on the false belief that he was more solidly based than was the case. He is now dependent on what remains of his core hard-left supporters plus the kneejerk Labour voters — the 18 per cent identified in the *Times*/YouGov poll (report, Jul 4).
Alan Cropper
London SE12

Sir, The latest UK-wide YouGov poll for *The Times* raises urgent questions about Westminster's archaic electoral system. With four parties on about 20 per cent of the vote, voters' representation is just a few percentage points between either annihilation at the next election or winning an unfair landslide. This absurd instability means that it is in the national interest to back a democratic, proportional voting system that guarantees voters fair results and co-operation. With the present electoral system millions of people are likely to feel forced to vote tactically rather than for their first choice, and vote-splitting may lead to unprecedented volatility and random results. Far from being a "strong and stable" system, first past the post is now an engine of uncertainty.
Jess Blair
Electoral Reform Society

Sir, David Aaronovitch's article and your report "Labour poll support at record low" highlight what has become obvious to most of us but not, apparently, to the two main political parties: a general election in the autumn is now highly likely but a majority win for any one party is not. The most probable outcome is a five-way split, with the SNP winning most of Scotland on 50-plus seats, the pro-Brexit vote dividing between the Conservative Party and the Brexit Party, Labour fading further, and the Lib Dems gaining ground with Remainer support. As Aaronovitch says, the two-horse race days are gone. We are destined for a hung parliament unlike any other, with some form of cross-party alliance needed before any government can be formed.
Robert Drysdale
Edinburgh

Hunt's soundbites

Sir, The impotence of Britain in being unable to help the people of Hong Kong is brilliantly exposed by Peter Brookes's cartoon (Jul 3). Jeremy Hunt can huff and puff but the Chinese will pay him little attention. One of the many consequences of leaving the EU and the excellent trading arrangements that we have with our neighbours is that we will be alone in the world, separating ourselves from an economic superpower with the clout to influence others. The price to be paid for "taking back control" is that we will be forced to seek trading agreements with China and other unpleasant and tyrannical regimes that will readily penalise us if we have the temerity to criticise them.
Robert Elkeles
Northwood, Middx

BBC stars' pay rise

Sir, Perhaps a maximum annual salary of, say, £250,000 should be set for retained entertainers, pundits and certain other BBC staff (letter, Jul 4). If they disliked the rate they could ply their trade elsewhere. By any standard what is paid to the likes of Messrs Lineker, Norton, Edwards and Shearer must far exceed their real value to the BBC. I for one would not stop watching *Match of the Day* were it not presented by Messrs Lineker and Shearer. Indeed, *MotD* without either might be more attractive. There must be many other presenters out there who are just as capable (if not more) and who are more than ready to appear for a much smaller reward.
Philip Dimond
Otham, Kent

that distort the earning figures of some of the highest-paid presenters. This is especially important given the decision to remove free TV licences for all those aged over 75.
The BBC is a publicly funded organisation, and as such should not pay inflated salaries.
Tom Hendry
Salisbury

End-of-life care

Sir, The letter (Jul 3) from the palliative care consultant Dr Carol Davis states that if a dying patient wishes to end their life then those "involved in their care must ensure that they do everything to make their death dignified and peaceful". Just what does that mean if it is not assisting suicide for the terminally ill, even if it may extend over a rather

Fig 35

Lord Heseltine and the removal of the whip

Sir, The sheer folly of suspending Michael Heseltine from the Conservative whip defies both logic and belief. Michael has served the Conservative Party loyally and well for more than 40 years — in good days and bad. At a time of growing cynicism in politics, his convictions — his *Conservative* convictions — have remained solid, constant and true. Millions of Conservatives — myself included — share those convictions.

Withdrawing the whip from such a man — on an issue of conscience — is an over-reaction that will encourage many moderate Conservatives to follow Michael's example.

Who are these blinkered people who have suspended the whip from a lifelong servant of the party? Moreover, a servant who has contributed to the social and economic welfare of our country on a scale that his critics neither can — nor will — ever match.

I am not the only Conservative who will be dismayed by this decision, which highlights yet again how far our party is moving away from the compassionate and moderate One Nation policies that have enabled the Conservatives to dominate politics for so long. If the views of the Michael Heseltines of our party are no longer tolerated within it, then our party has truly lost its way.

Sir John Major
Prime minister 1990-97, London SW1

Sir, Lord Heseltine deserves gratitude from all of us for speaking out against the folly of Brexit and the huge damage and division that the whole process continues to inflict on our country. He has put country before party, as should all moderate Tory and Labour MPs. What a pity he cannot lead the Tory party.

Robert Elkeles
Northwood, Middx

Sir, How I wish that your leading article "Road to Nowhere" (May 20) could be nightly reading for every Conservative Party member. Those same members seem likely to vote in the very man I blame for much of the present debacle: Boris Johnson. He took several days to decide if he was more likely to be PM as a Brexiteer or a Remainer; you are to be congratulated for speaking so plainly.

Despite being a lifelong Conservative voter, I will not be voting Tory next time (and not, of course, for Labour).

Barry McDonald
Stratford-upon-Avon

Sir, Rachel Sylvester (Comment, M 21) complains of a "profound" lack democracy in the Conservative Party's process of electing its leade Few methods could have been mo profoundly democratic than that u by the Labour Party in selecting its own. Where has that led?

Roland Shepherd
Gospel Green, Surrey

Sir, It seems unjust that a case of throwing a milkshake at a politicia being actively pursued by the polic given that they sometimes regard common assault as too minor to investigate. And by telling a fast-fo outlet not to sell a product because customer might throw it, they appe to have exceeded their powers. The time would be better spent pursuin extreme Brexiteers who make deat threats to MPs than disgruntled Remainers who merely embarrass self-important politicians.

James Shillady
London SW15

Fig 36

CHAPTER 15

Reflections

I have, on the whole, been very fortunate and have not had to endure the life-changing events encountered by my parents. They were very grateful to Britain for allowing them to settle and remained so for the rest of their lives. I too have enjoyed the benefits of living here and never cease to be grateful for life in Britain. It is hard to imagine what the Jews in Nazi Germany must have endured. To find yourselves as outcasts in the country in which you live must be devastating. I am always amazed at how few people appreciate what a great country this is in which to live. We have a relatively stable political situation, law and order with a judiciary of high standards and free from corruption, tolerance, freedom of speech, welfare benefits and an NHS, stable climate and much else. People from all over the world sacrifice everything to come here. Yet so many people fail to appreciate the quality of life here.

As I write this, we live in the midst of a worldwide pandemic of coronavirus, which has severely affected our country as well as most others. We are having to get used to a new way of life which seems likely to last for the foreseeable future. I am very concerned about the huge increase in unemployment which will shortly hit us.

At this difficult time in our history the country should be pulling together as one. A good example of the unnecessary divisions are those caused by Scottish nationalists, who spew out vitriol against all things English. They seem to think that they would be so much happier if an independent nation. It is hard to imagine what sort of paradise they could create by independence. Economically they are likely to be worse off. We are clearly far better off together in our United Kingdom. It is ironic that people from Europe, the Middle East, Africa, struggle to come and live in the UK. If you listened to the Scottish nationalists, you would imagine that they are an oppressed nation. In fact, they do well as part of the UK. However, if and when they have a vote, the outcome will likely be decided on emotion. I pointed this out in a letter to *The Times*, August 30th 2014 (Fig 34).

One factor weighing heavily with the Scots is the decision by the United Kingdom to leave the EU and I can sympathise with the Scots on this point. Britain voted by a narrow margin to leave whereas the Scots voted to remain. The whole Brexit process has been hugely damaging and divisive for our country. From the time before the referendum and in the years after, nearly all the government's attention and energy has been focussed on Brexit, to the detriment of many other important issues such as social care, crime, health, education etc. The whole country, and indeed, families, were divided. Rather like the Scots and their independence, much was left to emotion. The population fell under the sway of a demagogue, Nigel Farage, who has a very loud voice and campaigned incessantly, telling people how bad Europe was for us. Although not nearly as evil as Adolf Hitler, the principle of the oratory was the same. If you tell lies often enough, people will believe them. People were told that once out of Europe we could spend an extra £350million a week on the NHS. This figure has never been substantiated. We were told we would be overrun by people from Turkey and that 500 million people from the EU would have the right to settle here. We were told that we were being governed by unelected bureaucrats from Brussels. Now we seem to be run by an unelected prime ministerial advisor, Dominic Cummings. There is much wrong with the EU: the Euro, the Common Agricultural Policy etc. However, common sense dictates that we need to trade with countries close by. To cut ourselves off from the biggest market in the world, of 500 million people, seems an act of pure folly.

Brexiteers kept telling us that we would now be able to trade globally. I could never quite understand with whom. China was, of course, one of their main targets. We have rather belatedly found out how dangerous China is, especially in her treatment of the citizens of Hong Kong. When the then foreign secretary, Jeremy Hunt, protested to China about their reaction to the Hong Kong demonstrations in favour of freedom, I pointed out in a letter to *The Times*, July 5th 2019 (Fig 35) that he could huff and puff but the Chinese would take no notice, especially as we were so weak economically, having cut ourselves off from the economic superpower of Europe.

Brexiteers thought a trade deal with the USA would be straightforward. It never was likely to be and dealing with president Trump has proven a nightmare. If the Democrats win the next Presidential vote, we are not likely to be favoured in trade. There are big problems with USA agricultural husbandry standards for us. All the farmers who voted to leave the EU are now protesting that they will be undercut by cheap USA produce. An area such as Sunderland voted strongly to leave. Yet, the chief executive of the Nissan car plant, the major employer in the area, has stated that without a trade deal with Europe they will not be viable, and all these workers could lose their jobs. Wales too has benefited enormously from European grants, yet the Welsh voted to leave. One of the slogans of Brexiteers was to "take back control". A trade deal with the USA, if achieved, will likely place the USA in control.

Our politics has been poisoned and polarised by the Brexit issue. Many of the best and most competent Tories were "Remainers" and were deselected because they resisted the so-called "will of the people". Lord Heseltine, who had been deputy prime minister in Margaret Thatcher's time, had long spoken out against the folly of leaving the EU. The Tory whip was removed from him in the House of Lords. I wrote in his defence to *The Times* on May 22nd 2019, as did Sir John Major (Fig 36).

Our politics also suffered from a completely useless and ineffective opposition. The Labour Party elected Jeremy Corbyn to be their leader. Although during the referendum campaign he pretended to want to remain, in reality he did not like the EU as it was too capitalist. He was ineffective during the campaign and thereafter. If we had had an effective opposition, we probably would not have left the EU. His tenure as leader was also tainted by antisemitism, which really upset the Jewish community here. Happily, he was replaced.

The vast majority of economists think that the economy will suffer from leaving the EU. Writing in the *Financial Times* (December 11th 2018), Sir Mark Boleat, previously chair of the City of London policy and resources committee and a personal friend, wrote that our exit from Europe would result in the loss of many tens of thousands of jobs in the City and cost £billions in lost tax revenue.

There are many other downsides to leaving the EU. Sir Paul Nurse, who heads the world-class Francis Crick Institute, Britain's largest biomedical research institute, said that failure to continue to get access to Europe's flagship Horizon programme will mean the loss of £billions in research grants, which we were very successful in winning. It would be likely that we would drop out of the "Champions league of science". Our own MP, David Gauke, who had held several cabinet posts, including secretary of state for justice, was a committed Remainer and thus disliked by the local party. He campaigned hard against a "no deal" Brexit. There was a move in the local party to deselect him. We attended the meeting called to do this. I and others spoke in his defence. I made the point about the detrimental effect leaving the EU with no deal would have on British science. I was booed by some members of the audience. This was the level of ignorance displayed by many people. My view was that it would have been better to stay in the EU and try to change it from within with our considerable diplomatic skills and influence. This of course might have been difficult.

On the other side of the argument there is strong impetus within the EU for more integration and a European state, about which Britain has never felt comfortable. Perhaps, after all, Brexit may work out for us. Gideon Rachman, writing in the *Financial Times* on August 3rd 2020, suggested that the UK could form a new relationship with the EU similar to that between Canada and the USA. We need the EU as a partner to deal with threats beyond Europe, such as China. If we had a special relationship with the EU as well as the USA, the UK could be back at the centre of a reinvigorated Western alliance.

An effective Western alliance is sorely needed. At present the world is dominated by two malevolent superpowers, China and Russia, and the currently dysfunctional USA under Donald Trump. Only fairly recently have we woken up to the evils of China. Only a few years ago, Prime Minister David Cameron and Chancellor George Osborne hailed a "golden age of UK-China co-operation". We now find that China is persecuting its Uighur Muslim population, locking them up in so-called "education centres" or concentration camps. Strangely, there seems to be almost no protest about these horrors from the rest of the world's Muslims. Similarly, as the nationalist government of India discriminates against its country's Muslims, there is no worldwide Muslim protest. This is in stark contrast to worldwide protests at any action by Israel against Palestinians.

The Chinese are forcibly acquiring territory in the South China Sea, depriving people in Hong Kong of their previously agreed democratic rights, making aggressive noises against Taiwan and using their economic power to influence nations throughout the world. They are hacking into our industry and security systems etc. This is the country our Brexiteers thought would partly replace the EU as a main trading partner. The Russians, under Mr Putin, dispose of any internal dissent and pursue dissenters around the world, poisoning Alexander Litvinenko and Julia and Sergei Skripal in Salisbury, and others. The main opposition leader in Russia, Alexei Navalny, was fighting for his life in a Berlin hospital, having apparently been poisoned with Novichok nerve poison. He has now been discharged. Seeking to establish Russia as a world power, Putin has propped up the corrupt Assad regime in Syria, which has destroyed the country, and killed hundreds of thousands of people and rendered millions homeless.

The USA has been ineffective under Donald Trump and is no longer leading the democratic Western world. Beside these are countries like Iran, which seeks to gain power by spreading terrorism, and Turkey, ruled by a dictator obsessed by his own absolute power, who has imprisoned more journalists than most other countries. Saudi Arabia is ruled by a ruthless royal involved in assassination. Many African states are ruled by corrupt dictators. Much international aid is siphoned off by these people, stifling progress. The appalling Robert Mugabe in Zimbabwe has been replaced by Emmerson Mnangagwa, who seems even worse. True democracy in the world seems to be under threat. Countries in Eastern Europe such as Hungary and Poland are under the influence of politicians who are seeking to limit democracy. The hope, therefore, of anything useful coming out of the United Nations is non-existent. Any constructive resolution of the Security Council is blocked by Russia or China or both. When a disaster strikes, the UK, France and USA are usually to be found helping but the Russians and Chinese are nowhere. Currently Beirut in the Lebanon has been paralysed by a massive explosion which has destroyed much of the city. So far, no Arab countries, many of whom have great wealth, have offered to help.

There are now relatively few countries in which people can live in safety or security. Hence there is a tide of migrants from Africa, the Middle East and Afghanistan trying to escape into Europe, and especially the UK. This is a massive problem to which currently there appears no solution.

Where does all this leave us in the UK? Despite the fact that we are one of the most tolerant of all societies, we flagellate ourselves in the so-called Black Lives Matter campaign, blaming current society for the story of our Empire. The finding that those in the Black and Asian minority groups seem to have had higher mortality in the current Covid crisis is used as an example of our discrimination against them, even though multiple factors are likely to be involved. As a country we have been greatly weakened and divided by the whole Brexit process. Even now we do not know what our relationship will be to the EU. We certainly need a deal which will enable us to trade freely and seamlessly with our neighbours. Currently, we are both weak and isolated. We have antagonised the Scots and the EU and our special relationship with the USA seems illusory. We quarrel with France over the continuing flow of migrants from French shores to our own. Sir Max Hastings recently wrote in *The Times* that our 'lap dog cabinet is the weakest in a century'. They were chosen because of loyalty to the prime minister, Boris Johnson, and to Brexit. We have lived through very difficult times, which would be a challenge for any competent government.

We need to pull together. We need to appreciate all that is good in our country. For instance, we have led the world in scientific discoveries for treatment of the coronavirus. We need to persuade the Scots that they would be better off staying in the UK, although this will be difficult. We should form a firm alliance with the EU so that we can better influence the world and be an effective force for good.

For myself, I feel that I have achieved what I set out to do. I do not think that I would in retrospect change any of the decisions which I have made. I cannot pretend that I have had a big influence on events. However, I believe that I have helped many in the course of my work and life.

As I write, I have just had a very unpleasant few weeks. On July 6th I had a routine cataract operation on my right eye. Both my optician and ophthalmologist advised me to proceed with this. I was reluctant because I felt my eyesight was reasonable. They said that I would be borderline for driving. Everyone whom I know who has had the procedure had no problems. The morning after the procedure, when I removed the eye patch as instructed, I could see nothing through the eye. This was truly frightening. I saw the specialist two days later, who said I had a very rare complication of the operation called "macular oedema", which is fluid accumulation around the nerves of central vision at the back of the eye. He confirmed this with an eye scan and prescribed anti-inflammatory drops. I had lost central vision in the eye. It was like looking into a dense fog. There was slight improvement over the next three weeks until I saw him again. I had another scan, and he said the scan appearances had improved and he could not understand why I had so much loss of vision. Because, since then, I had been able to see little more, he recommended that I have a fluorescein angiogram to look at the blood vessels at the back of the eye. I was referred to another specialist who concluded that I had suffered a "retinal ischaemic event", a sort of mini-stroke, during the procedure and that my vision would not improve further. I have seen a further specialist who thought that something happened during the procedure to raise the pressure in the eye, causing loss of blood supply to part of the retina, possibly related to the local anaesthetic. This seems more likely to me. This apparently is incredibly rare, and I have been exceptionally unlucky. I retain peripheral vision in the eye but anything straight in front is a fog and I cannot read with it. As you can imagine, this has been a major blow to me, as one who has worked hard during my life to keep physically fit. The message from all this is, do not have any procedure or operation unless it is really necessary.

Finally, I would like to express my appreciation to this country. It gave refuge to my parents and allowed them to live in peace, security and prosperity. They really enjoyed their lives here. I too have benefitted hugely from living in this country. I have had a fulfilling professional life and have met many wonderful people, both in my work and leisure activities. To all of them I am very grateful.

I should like to conclude by expressing my huge appreciation to Arran, my wife and life companion, to whom I owe so much.